MAX LUCADO

LIFE LESSONS *from*

1 & 2 THESSALONIANS

Transcendent Living in a Transient World

PREPARED BY THE LIVINGSTONE CORPORATION

THOMAS NELSON
Since 1798

Published in Nashville, Tennessee, by Thomas Nelson. Thomas Nelson is a registered trademark of HarperCollins Christian Publishing, Inc.

Produced with the assistance of the Livingstone Corporation. Project staff include Jake Barton, Joel Bartlett, Andy Culbertson, Will Reaves, Mary Horner Collins, and Rachel Hawkins

Editor: Len Woods

First Printing October 2018 / Printed in the United States of America

CONTENTS

HOW TO STUDY THE BIBLE

The Bible is a peculiar book. Words crafted in another language. Deeds done in a distant era. Events recorded in a far-off land. Counsel offered to a foreign people. It is a peculiar book.

It's surprising that anyone reads it. It's too old. Some of its writings date back 5,000 years. It's too bizarre. The book speaks of incredible floods, fires, earthquakes, and people with supernatural abilities. It's too radical. The Bible calls for undying devotion to a carpenter who called himself God's Son.

Logic says this book shouldn't survive. Too old, too bizarre, too radical.

The Bible has been banned, burned, scoffed, and ridiculed. Scholars have mocked it as foolish. Kings have branded it as illegal. A thousand times over the grave has been dug and the dirge has begun, but somehow the Bible never stays in the grave. Not only has it survived, but it has also thrived. It is the single most popular book in all of history. It has been the bestselling book in the world for years!

There is no way on earth to explain it. Which perhaps is the only explanation. For the Bible's durability is not found on *earth* but in *heaven*. The millions who have tested its claims and claimed its promises know there is but one answer: the Bible is God's book and God's voice.

As you read it, you would be wise to give some thought to two questions: *What is the purpose of the Bible?* and *How do I study the Bible?* Time spent reflecting on these two issues will greatly enhance your Bible study.

What is the purpose of the Bible?

Let the Bible itself answer that question: *"From infancy you have known the Holy Scriptures, which are able to make you wise for salvation through faith in Christ Jesus"* (2 Timothy 3:15).

The purpose of the Bible? Salvation. God's highest passion is to get his children home. His book, the Bible, describes his plan of salvation. The purpose of the Bible is to proclaim God's plan and passion to save his children.

This is the reason why this book has endured through the centuries. It dares to tackle the toughest questions about life: *Where do I go after I die? Is there a God? What do I do with my fears?* The Bible is the treasure map that leads to God's highest treasure—eternal life.

But how do you study the Bible? Countless copies of Scripture sit unread on bookshelves and nightstands simply because people don't know how to read it. What can you do to make the Bible real in your life?

The clearest answer is found in the words of Jesus: *"Ask and it will be given to you; seek and you will find; knock and the door will be opened to you"* (Matthew 7:7).

The first step in understanding the Bible is asking God to help you. You should read it prayerfully. If anyone understands God's Word, it is because of God and not the reader.

"The Advocate, the Holy Spirit, whom the Father will send in my name, will teach you all things and will remind you of everything I have said to you" (John 14:26).

Before reading the Bible, pray and invite God to speak to you. Don't go to Scripture looking for your idea, but go searching for his.

Not only should you read the Bible prayerfully, but you should also read it carefully. *"Seek and you will find"* is the pledge. The Bible is not a newspaper to be skimmed but rather a mine to be quarried. *"If you look for it as for silver and search for it as for hidden treasure, then you will understand the fear of the LORD and find the knowledge of God"* (Proverbs 2:4–5).

Any worthy find requires effort. The Bible is no exception. To understand the Bible, you don't have to be brilliant, but you must be willing to roll up your sleeves and search.

"Do your best to present yourself to God as one approved, a worker who does not need to be ashamed and who correctly handles the word of truth" (2 Timothy 2:15).

Here's a practical point. Study the Bible a bit at a time. Hunger is not satisfied by eating twenty-one meals in one sitting once a week. The body needs a steady diet to remain strong. So does the soul. When God sent food to his people in the wilderness, he didn't provide loaves already made. Instead, he sent them manna in the shape of *"thin flakes like frost on the ground"* (Exodus 16:14).

God gave manna in limited portions.

God sends spiritual food the same way. He opens the heavens with just enough nutrients for today's hunger. He provides *"a rule for this, a rule for that; a little here, a little there"* (Isaiah 28:10).

Don't be discouraged if your reading reaps a small harvest. Some days a lesser portion is all that is needed. What is important is to search every day for that day's message. A steady diet of God's Word over a lifetime builds a healthy soul and mind.

It's much like the little girl who returned from her first day at school feeling a bit dejected. Her mom asked, "Did you learn anything?"

"Apparently not enough," the girl responded. "I have to go back tomorrow, and the next day, and the next . . . "

Such is the case with learning. And such is the case with Bible study. Understanding comes little by little over a lifetime.

There is a third step in understanding the Bible. After the asking and seeking comes the knocking. After you ask and search, *"knock and the door will be opened to you"* (Matthew 7:7).

To knock is to stand at God's door. To make yourself available. To climb the steps, cross the porch, stand at the doorway, and volunteer. Knocking goes beyond the realm of thinking and into the realm of acting.

To knock is to ask, *What can I do? How can I obey? Where can I go?*

It's one thing to know what to do. It's another to do it. But for those who do it—those who choose to obey—a special reward awaits them.

"Whoever looks intently into the perfect law that gives freedom, and continues in it—not forgetting what they have heard, but doing it—they will be blessed in what they do" (James 1:25).

What a promise. Blessings come to those who do what they read in God's Word! It's the same with medicine. If you only read the label but ignore the pills, it won't help. It's the same with food. If you only read the recipe but never cook, you won't be fed. And it's the same with the Bible. If you only read the words but never obey, you'll never know the joy God has promised.

Ask. Search. Knock. Simple, isn't it? So why don't you give it a try? If you do, you'll see why the Bible is the most remarkable book in history.

The Books of 1 and 2 Thessalonians

1 THESSALONIANS

Saint Cyprian, a bishop of Carthage in the third century and a notable early Christian author, wrote the following to a friend named Donatus:

What a compliment! *A quiet and holy people.* Is there any phrase that captures the essence of the faith any better? *A quiet and holy people.*

Quiet.

Not obnoxious. Not boastful. Not demanding. Just quiet. Contagiously quiet.

Holy.

Set apart. Pure. Decent. Honest. Wholesome. Holy. A quiet and holy people.

Paul urges the same from us. "Make it your ambition to lead a quiet life: You should mind your own business and work with your hands, just as we told you, so that your daily life may win the respect of outsiders and so that you will not be dependent on anybody" (1 Thessalonians 4:11–12).

A quiet and holy people. That describes the church in Thessalonica. May that describe the church today.

AUTHOR AND DATE

Paul, who persecuted the early church before his life was radically altered by meeting the risen Jesus on the road to Damascus (see Acts 9:1–31). Paul founded the church at Thessalonica, located in the Roman province of Macedonia, during his second missionary journey (c. AD 50), after being pressured by officials in Philippi to leave that city (see 16:38–17:4). Many people there accepted Paul's message, but after some time a group of Jews in the city instigated a riot, and ultimately the believers sent Paul and Silas away to Berea (see 17:5–10). It is likely that Paul wrote his first letter to the Thessalonian believers from the city of Corinth later that same year.

SITUATION

After fleeing to Berea, Paul journeyed to Athens and then to Corinth (see Acts 17:15–18:1). While he was there, he received a report from his co-worker Timothy about the status of the believers that he had been forced to leave behind in Thessalonica. The report so encouraged Paul that he immediately wrote his first letter to them (see 1 Thessalonians 3:6–7). In addition to expressing his praise to God for the healthy condition of the church, Paul appears to have written the letter to (1) counter false claims against him and his associates, (2) suggest ways the believers could continue to grow spiritually, and (3) clear up misunderstandings the believers had about the nature and timing of Jesus' return to this world.

KEY THEMES

- We should live in preparation for Christ's return.
- God wants holy and pure worship.
- The time of Christ's return will be unpredictable.
- How we live our everyday lives, matters.

KEY VERSES

Rejoice always, pray continually, give thanks in all circumstances; for this is God's will for you in Christ Jesus (1 Thessalonians 5:16–18).

CONTENTS

2 THESSALONIANS

I'm seated on an airplane. A grounded airplane. I'm surrounded by kids. Restless kids.

The kids are mine. The plane is not. The plane is late, however, and my kids are restless. I took them with me on a trip so we'd have a bit of time together. This is more than I had in mind.

They ask the questions you'd expect of a five-year-old and eight-year-old. "Are they bringing drinks yet?"

"When are we going to leave?"

"How much more time?"

"Are we nearly home?"

"Why is it taking so long?"

Questions. Lots of questions. The kind of questions that were circulating through the church at Thessalonica. They, too, were restless. Somewhere they got the idea that Jesus was returning tomorrow, so they got ready. Some were selling their homes, others were quitting their work, and all were twiddling their thumbs while awaiting the return of Christ.

Paul gets wind of their assumption and writes them this letter. He urges them not to buy into the reports that the final days have already begun. Several things still need to occur first, and until they do, their task is to be patient and alert.

No easy task. Human nature tends to be one or the other. We tend to be so patient we aren't alert, or so alert we aren't patient. The church becomes the hybrid of the restless and the resting. The result can be squabbling kids. Just like mine. They've done their best to be patient, but after a while a person can only take so much.

"Hang in there," I say.

"We'll be home soon," I urge.

"Try to get along," I exhort.

(I'm starting to sound a lot like Paul.)

AUTHOR AND DATE

Paul is believed to have written 2 Thessalonians shortly after composing his first letter to the believers in this Macedonian city whom he had been abruptly forced to leave behind (c. AD 51). It appears he was still ministering in the city of Corinth when he received further word—this time from an unknown source—about the condition of the believers' faith in Thessalonica. These updates prompted him to write his second letter as a follow-up to his first to address other issues and concerns that had arisen in the young but growing Christian community.

SITUATION

Paul's first letter to the Thessalonians had evidently been well received by the believers. They were satisfied with Paul's explanation about those in the faith who had died and were remaining true to the gospel that he had preached to them. However, it appears that persecution against the believers had grown worse in the city, and false doctrines were circulating that the events of Jesus' return and the end-times were already in progress. As a result, many of the believers were avoiding their vocational responsibilities, which was creating a burden for those who were working. Paul sought to address these issues in this letter.

KEY THEMES

- With Jesus' return will come accountability.
- We should stay busy with obedient lives until Christ returns.
- We must keep our beliefs, our doctrines, pure.

KEY VERSE

But we ought always to thank God for you, brothers and sisters loved by the Lord, because God chose you as firstfruits to be saved through the sanctifying work of the Spirit and through belief in the truth (2 Thessalonians 2:13).

CONTENTS

TRUE TRANSFORMATION

*We give thanks to God always for you all, making
mention of you in our prayers, remembering
without ceasing your work of faith, labor of love,
and patience of hope in our Lord Jesus Christ.*
1 THESSALONIANS 1:2–3 NKJV

REFLECTION

It's been said that the only two certainties in life are death and taxes. But we could add another item to that list—*change*. Think about it. Nothing in this world stays the same. Emotions vacillate. Relationships fluctuate. Material things deteriorate. Look at your own life. What are some of the primary things in your life that are different now than they were ten years ago?

SITUATION

The city of Thessalonica was a major trade center in the ancient world with an excellent natural harbor. In Paul's day it attracted a number of Jewish merchants, and a synagogue had been built there. This building offered Paul an obvious place to begin to share the gospel, and both Jews and Gentiles came to believe in Christ—including a man named Jason, who allowed Paul to stay in his home. Yet Paul's success angered certain other Jews of the city, and the apostle and his team ultimately were forced to leave. When Paul later received a favorable report on the status of the church, he immediately wrote a letter to encourage the believers to persevere and continue to allow God to bring about the transformation he had begun in their lives.

OBSERVATION

Read 1 Thessalonians 1:1–10 from the New International Version or the New King James Version.

NEW INTERNATIONAL VERSION

[1] Paul, Silas and Timothy,

To the church of the Thessalonians in God the Father and the Lord Jesus Christ:

Grace and peace to you.

[2] We always thank God for all of you and continually mention you in our prayers. [3] We remember before our God and Father your work produced by faith, your labor prompted by love, and your endurance inspired by hope in our Lord Jesus Christ.

[4] For we know, brothers and sisters loved by God, that he has chosen you, [5] because our gospel came to you not simply with words but also with power, with the Holy Spirit and deep conviction. You know how we lived among you for your sake. [6] You became imitators of us

and of the Lord, for you welcomed the message in the midst of severe suffering with the joy given by the Holy Spirit.[7] And so you became a model to all the believers in Macedonia and Achaia. [8] The Lord's message rang out from you not only in Macedonia and Achaia—your faith in God has become known everywhere. Therefore we do not need to say anything about it, [9] for they themselves report what kind of reception you gave us. They tell how you turned to God from idols to serve the living and true God, [10] and to wait for his Son from heaven, whom he raised from the dead—Jesus, who rescues us from the coming wrath.

New King James Version

[1] Paul, Silvanus, and Timothy,

To the church of the Thessalonians in God the Father and the Lord Jesus Christ:

Grace to you and peace from God our Father and the Lord Jesus Christ.

[2] We give thanks to God always for you all, making mention of you in our prayers, [3] remembering without ceasing your work of faith, labor of love, and patience of hope in our Lord Jesus Christ in the sight of our God and Father, [4] knowing, beloved brethren, your election by God. [5] For our gospel did not come to you in word only, but also in power, and in the Holy Spirit and in much assurance, as you know what kind of men we were among you for your sake.

[6] And you became followers of us and of the Lord, having received the word in much affliction, with joy of the Holy Spirit, [7] so that you became examples to all in Macedonia and Achaia who believe. [8] For from you the word of the Lord has sounded forth, not only in Macedonia and Achaia, but also in every place. Your faith toward God has gone out, so that we do not need to say anything. [9] For they themselves declare concerning us what manner of entry we had to you, and how you turned to God from idols to serve the living and true God, [10] and to wait for His Son from heaven, whom He raised from the dead, even Jesus who delivers us from the wrath to come.

EXPLORATION

1. Read about the founding of the church at Thessalonica in Acts 17:1–9. How does the beginning of their community compare with the history of your church?

_____

_____

_____

_____

_____

_____

_____

2. What are some reasons Paul gives for being thankful for the believers in Thessalonica?

_____

_____

_____

_____

_____

_____

3. What do you think Paul means when he says that God "chose" the believers?

_____

_____

_____

_____

_____

_____

4. How does Paul describe the gospel that he presented to them? Why do you think he stresses the message he delivered was not "in word only, but also in power" (verse 5)?

_____

_____

_____

_____

_____

_____

5. In what ways were the believers in Thessalonica an example to the other churches?

_____

_____

_____

_____

_____

_____

6. Which is more important—a transformed character or a rock-solid reputation? Why?

_____

_____

_____

_____

_____

_____

INSPIRATION

Here is (dare I say it?) the greatest miracle of God. It is astounding when God heals the body. It is extraordinary when God hears the prayer. It is incredible when God provides the new job, the new car, the new child. But none of these compares to when God creates new life.

At our new birth God remakes our souls and gives us what we need, again. New eyes so we can see by faith. A new mind so we can have the mind of Christ. New strength so we won't grow tired. A new vision so we won't lose heart. A new voice for praise and new hands for service. And most of all, a new heart. A heart that has been cleansed by Christ.

And, oh, how we need it. We have soiled what he gave us the first time. We have used our eyes to see impurity, our hands to give pain, our feet to walk the wrong path, our minds to think evil thoughts. All of us need to be made new again.

The first birth was for earthly life; the second one is for eternal life. The first time we received a physical heart; the second time we receive a spiritual heart. The first birth enabled us to have life on earth. The second birth enables us to have life eternal. (From *A Gentle Thunder* by Max Lucado.)

REACTION

7. What were the circumstances surrounding your decision to accept Christ as your Savior?

_____

_____

_____

_____

_____

_____

8. What prompted you to listen to the messengers who first explained the gospel to you?

_____

_____

_____

_____

_____

9. What are the unmistakable signs that Christ has made you a new creature—that the Spirit of God lives in you?

_____

_____

_____

_____

_____

10. In what ways do you feel that you are an example to other believers?

_____

_____

_____

_____

_____

11. When other people discuss your faith, what do you suspect they say about you, about God, and about the church?

_____

_____

_____

_____

12. What areas of your life do you sense God's Spirit prompting you to examine?

_____

_____

_____

_____

_____

_____

_____

_____

LIFE LESSONS

Here's an arresting truth: we each have a reputation. Good or bad, everyone who is acquainted with us has an opinion about us. If our name comes up in conversation, people remember interactions and incidents they have had with us. If we are not around, they may say things about us—either good ("she is one of the kindest people I know"), or bad ("Oh, yeah, him . . . he's a self-absorbed jerk"). The fact is, if we claim to be followers of Jesus, our reputation is enormously important. So, how do we go about making ours better? Not by working on our *image* but by focusing on our *character*. When we let God do his transforming work in our hearts, the difference Christ makes will slowly become evident on the surface of our lives.

DEVOTION

Father, thank you for the great hope of the gospel—that we don't have to stay as we are. We can change, by the power of your Spirit. Work in us. Show us the inconsistencies in our lives. Help us to be a better example to those around us today.

JOURNALING

In what ways do you see God gradually transforming your heart and your mind?

_____

_____

_____

_____

_____

_____

_____

_____

_____

_____

_____

_____

_____

_____

_____

_____

_____

_____

_____

_____

_____

_____

FOR FURTHER READING

To complete the books of 1 and 2 Thessalonians during this twelve-part study, read 1 Thessalonians 1:1–10. For more Bible passages on the need to live transformed lives, read Daniel 1:8; Matthew 5:13–16; Acts 5:20; 1 Timothy 6:18; and 1 Peter 2:12; 3:15.

LESSON TWO

THE QUESTION OF MOTIVES

For the appeal we make does not spring from error or impure motives, nor are we trying to trick you. On the contrary, we speak as those approved by God to be entrusted with the gospel.

1 THESSALONIANS 2:3–4

REFLECTION

It isn't enough to merely do the right things. The Bible makes it clear that God not only cares about *what* we do but also *why* we do it. Take a few moments to ponder your own heart in each of these areas: Why do you go to church? Why do you hang out with the friends you have chosen? What are your motives for working where you do and the way you do?

SITUATION

Paul, having explained why he was thankful for the Thessalonian believers, now expresses one of the primary purposes for writing his letter: to defend his motives for the work he did when he was with them. It appears that after Paul left Thessalonica, he became the target of multiple accusations in this regard. The identity of these opponents is not known, but they could have been pagan Gentiles who lived in the area or the relentless band of hostile Jews who shadowed his movements. Paul responds to these false accusations by explaining his *true* motives.

OBSERVATION

Read 1 Thessalonians 2:1–12 from the New International Version or the New King James Version.

NEW INTERNATIONAL VERSION

[1] You know, brothers and sisters, that our visit to you was not without results. [2] We had previously suffered and been treated outrageously in Philippi, as you know, but with the help of our God we dared to tell you his gospel in the face of strong opposition. [3] For the appeal we make does not spring from error or impure motives, nor are we trying to trick you. [4] On the contrary, we speak as those approved by God to be entrusted with the gospel. We are not trying to please people but God, who tests our hearts. [5] You know we never used flattery, nor did we put on a mask to cover up greed—God is our witness. [6] We were not looking for praise from people, not from you or anyone else, even though as apostles of Christ we could have asserted our authority. [7] Instead, we were like young children among you.

Just as a nursing mother cares for her children, [8] so we cared for you. Because we loved you so much, we were delighted to share with you not only the gospel of God but our lives as well. [9] Surely you remember, brothers and sisters, our toil and hardship; we worked night and day in order not to be a burden to anyone while we preached the gospel of God to you. [10] You are witnesses, and so is God, of how holy, righteous and blameless we were among you who believed. [11] For you know that we dealt with each of you as a father deals with his own children, [12] encouraging, comforting and urging you to live lives worthy of God, who calls you into his kingdom and glory.

New King James Version

[1] For you yourselves know, brethren, that our coming to you was not in vain. [2] But even after we had suffered before and were spitefully treated at Philippi, as you know, we were bold in our God to speak to you the gospel of God in much conflict. [3] For our exhortation did not come from error or uncleanness, nor was it in deceit.

[4] But as we have been approved by God to be entrusted with the gospel, even so we speak, not as pleasing men, but God who tests our hearts. [5] For neither at any time did we use flattering words, as you know, nor a cloak for covetousness—God is witness. [6] Nor did we seek glory from men, either from you or from others, when we might have made demands as apostles of Christ. [7] But we were gentle among you, just as a nursing mother cherishes her own children. [8] So, affectionately longing for you, we were well pleased to impart to you not only the gospel of God, but also our own lives, because you had become dear to us. [9] For you remember, brethren, our labor and toil; for laboring night and day, that we might not be a burden to any of you, we preached to you the gospel of God.

[10] You are witnesses, and God also, how devoutly and justly and blamelessly we behaved ourselves among you who believe; [11] as you know how we exhorted, and comforted, and charged every one of you, as a father does his own children, [12] that you would walk worthy of God who calls you into His own kingdom and glory.

EXPLORATION

1. Read about what Paul suffered in Philippi in Acts 16:16–24. Why do you think Paul reminds the Thessalonian believers of these events as he begins to defend his motives?

_____

_____

_____

_____

_____

2. How does Paul describe his motives in sharing the gospel with them (see verse 3)?

_____

_____

_____

_____

3. What is the advantage of being motivated solely by the goal of pleasing God? What are some ways that God "tests our hearts" in this (verse 4)?

_____

_____

_____

_____

4. What is Paul's point in using the analogies of motherhood and fatherhood in describing his interactions with the believers (see verses 7, 11–12)?

_____

_____

_____

_____

5. As you look at Paul's defense of his motives and ministry, can you echo those sentiments as you think back over your interactions with people from the last week? Why or why not?

_____

_____

_____

_____

_____

_____

6. Have you, like Paul, ever had someone question your motives? If so, how did you respond?

_____

_____

_____

_____

_____

INSPIRATION

When I learned that [my Dad] had a terminal disease, I wrote him, volunteering to change my plans and stay near him. He immediately wrote back, saying, "Don't be concerned about me. I have no fear of death or eternity; just go . . . please him."

My father's life is an example of a heart melted in the fire of God, formed on his anvil, and used in his vineyard. He knew, and knows, what his life was for. In a society of question and confusion, his was one life that had a definition.

Time on God's anvil should do that for us: It should clarify our mission and define our purpose. When a tool emerges from a blacksmith's anvil, there is no question as to what it is for. There is no question as to why it was made. One look at the tool and you instantly know its function. You pick up a hammer and you know that it was made to hit nails. You pick up a saw and you know that it was made to cut wood. You see a screwdriver and you know that it is for tightening screws.

As a human being emerges from the anvil of God, the same should be true. Being tested by God reminds us that our function and task is to be about his business, that our purpose is to be an extension of his nature, an ambassador of his throne room, and a proclaimer of his message. We should exit the shop with no question as to why God made us. We know our purpose. (From *Shaped by God* by Max Lucado.)

REACTION

7. When are some seasons in your life that you spent time on "God's anvil"? How did that serve to shape your goals and priorities?

_____

_____

_____

_____

_____

_____

8. How do you think the apostle Paul's "time on the anvil" shaped his purpose? How did this enable him to defend his motives when he was questioned?

_____

_____

_____

_____

_____

_____

9. Paul writes that he "could have asserted" his authority over the Thessalonians but instead chose to be "like young children" among them. Why do you think he took this approach?

_____

_____

_____

_____

_____

_____

10. What are some of the benefits of having a clear sense of God's calling on your life?

_____

_____

_____

_____

_____

11. The temptation to be a people pleaser is powerful. How can a believer in Christ realistically break free from this constant pressure?

_____

_____

_____

_____

_____

12. As you look at Paul's transparent discussion of his motives, what in particular stands out to you and challenges you to be different?

_____

_____

_____

_____

_____

LIFE LESSONS

Someone has observed that we can choose to fear God—and if so, we will fear *nothing* else. Or we can refuse to fear God—in which case, we will fear *everything* else. It is a life-changing moment when we realize God's opinion is the only thing that ultimately matters. When we get to that place, we find true freedom from the agendas of parents or peers. No more wringing our hands over what others think. We swap all those competing, confusing, crazy-making motivations for one simplified purpose: living to please God. We live our lives for an audience of one. Aren't you ready for such a life of simplicity, freedom, peace, and power?

DEVOTION

Heavenly Father, thank you for shaping us and giving us a clear purpose in this life. We know it is possible to be motivated purely by a love for you and a desire to honor you by serving others. That is was we want today. Give us the grace to find that simple and free life.

JOURNALING

What are some areas in my life where I have been seeking to please others instead of God?

_____

_____

_____

_____

_____

_____

_____

_____

_____

FOR FURTHER READING

To complete the books of 1 and 2 Thessalonians during this twelve-part study, read 1 Thessalonians 2:1–12. For more Bible passages on motives, read Proverbs 21:2; Matthew 6:1–2; 2 Corinthians 5:9–10; Galatians 1:10; Philippians 2:3; and Colossians 3:22.

WHEN HELL BREAKS LOOSE

*For you, brethren, became imitators of the churches of
God which are in Judea in Christ Jesus. For you also
suffered the same things from your own countrymen, just
as they did from the Judeans, who killed both the Lord
Jesus and their own prophets, and have persecuted us.*

1 THESSALONIANS 2:14–15 NKJV

REFLECTION

In his classic book *The Screwtape Letters*, C.S. Lewis warned of two possible errors in thinking about demons. On one extreme is the refusal to believe in their existence. On the other extreme is the equally dangerous mistake to "feel an excessive and unhealthy interest in them." Which of these tendencies do you most see in your own life? Explain.

SITUATION

Paul continues to defend his ministry by reminding the Thessalonians of the message he preached when he was with them—which they accepted as the word of God—and the powerful effect it had made on them. This is a message their enemy, "the god of this age" (2 Corinthians 4:4), did not want them to hear, and he was now doing all he could to cause them to abandon their faith. Paul acknowledges the believers have endured great persecution at the hands of others, but he compels them to continue on for Christ—for the day is coming when the wrath of God will come upon those who choose to reject the message of the gospel.

OBSERVATION

Read 1 Thessalonians 2:13–20 from the New International Version or the New King James Version.

NEW INTERNATIONAL VERSION

¹³ And we also thank God continually because, when you received the word of God, which you heard from us, you accepted it not as a human word, but as it actually is, the word of God, which is indeed at work in you who believe. ¹⁴ For you, brothers and sisters, became imitators of God's churches in Judea, which are in Christ Jesus: You suffered from your own people the same things those churches suffered from the Jews ¹⁵ who killed the Lord Jesus and the prophets and also drove us out. They displease God and are hostile to everyone ¹⁶ in their effort to keep us from speaking to the Gentiles so that they may be saved. In this way they always heap up their sins to the limit. The wrath of God has come upon them at last.

¹⁷ But, brothers and sisters, when we were orphaned by being separated from you for a short time (in person, not in thought), out of our intense longing we made every effort to see you. ¹⁸ For we wanted to come to you—certainly I, Paul, did, again and again—but Satan blocked our

way. ¹⁹ For what is our hope, our joy, or the crown in which we will glory in the presence of our Lord Jesus when he comes? Is it not you? ²⁰ Indeed, you are our glory and joy.

NEW KING JAMES VERSION

¹³ For this reason we also thank God without ceasing, because when you received the word of God which you heard from us, you welcomed it not as the word of men, but as it is in truth, the word of God, which also effectively works in you who believe. ¹⁴ For you, brethren, became imitators of the churches of God which are in Judea in Christ Jesus. For you also suffered the same things from your own countrymen, just as they did from the Judeans, ¹⁵ who killed both the Lord Jesus and their own prophets, and have persecuted us; and they do not please God and are contrary to all men, ¹⁶ forbidding us to speak to the Gentiles that they may be saved, so as always to fill up the measure of their sins; but wrath has come upon them to the uttermost.

¹⁷ But we, brethren, having been taken away from you for a short time in presence, not in heart, endeavored more eagerly to see your face with great desire. ¹⁸ Therefore we wanted to come to you—even I, Paul, time and again—but Satan hindered us. ¹⁹ For what is our hope, or joy, or crown of rejoicing? Is it not even you in the presence of our Lord Jesus Christ at His coming? ²⁰ For you are our glory and joy.

EXPLORATION

1. How does Paul describe the way in which the believers in Thessalonica received the message of the gospel? What does it mean when he says that message is "at work" in them (verse 13)?

_____

_____

_____

_____

_____

2. Based on this passage, what kind of opposition were the believers facing?

_____

_____

_____

_____

_____

3. What hope did Paul offer to the believers to encourage them to persevere in their faith?

_____

_____

_____

_____

4. In your life as a believer, when have you encountered the most opposition? What was the situation? How did you respond to that time of adversity?

_____

_____

_____

_____

5. Paul had evidently been accused of not caring for the Thessalonian believers or wanting to see them again. What does he reveal about the _true_ reasons for why he has not returned?

_____

_____

_____

_____

6. When are some times in your life that you have felt blocked from doing something God called you to do? How did you persevere through those difficult situations?

_____

_____

_____

_____

_____

_____

INSPIRATION

"If God is for us, who can be against us?" (Romans 8:31). The question is not simply, "Who can be against us?" You could answer that one. Who is against you? Disease, inflation, corruption, exhaustion. Calamities confront, and fears imprison. Were Paul's question, "Who can be against us?" we could list our foes much easier than we could fight them. But that is not the question. The question is, _If GOD is for us, who can be against us?_

Indulge me for a moment. Four words in this verse deserve your attention. Read slowly the phrase, "God is for us." Please pause for a minute before you continue. Read it again, aloud. (My apologies to the person next to you.) God is for us. Repeat the phrase four times, this time emphasizing each word. (Come on, you're not in that big of a hurry.)

God is for us.

God _is_ for us.

God is _for_ us.

God is for _us._

God is for you. Your parents may have forgotten you, your teachers may have neglected you, your siblings may be ashamed of you, but within reach of your prayers is the Maker of the oceans. God!

God *is* for you. Not "may be," not "has been," not "was," not "would be," but "God is!" He is for you. Today. At this hour. At this minute. As you read this sentence. No need to wait in line or come back tomorrow. He is with you. He could not be closer than he is at this second. His loyalty won't increase if you are better nor lessen if you are worse. He is for you.

God is *for* you. Turn to the sidelines; that's God cheering your run. Look past the finish line; that's God applauding your steps. Listen for him in the bleachers, shouting your name. Too tired to continue? He'll carry you. Too discouraged to fight? He's picking you up. God is for you.

God is for *you*. Had he a calendar, your birthday would be circled. If he drove a car, your name would be on his bumper. If there's a tree in heaven, he's carved your name in the bark. We know he has a tattoo, and we know what it says. "I have engraved you on the palms of my hands," he declares (Isaiah 49:16) . . .

God is with you. Knowing that, who is against you? Can death harm you now? Can disease rob your life? Can your purpose be taken or your value diminished? No. Though hell itself may set itself against you, no one can defeat you. You are protected. God is with you. (From *In the Grip of Grace* by Max Lucado.)

REACTION

7. Reflect on those four words from Paul: "God is for us" (Romans 8:31). When is it the hardest for you to believe that God is *for* you? Why?

_____

_____

_____

_____

_____

_____

8. What are some ways you can see God is *for* you even in the midst of your current struggles?

_____

_____

_____

_____

_____

_____

9. What are some of the more effective tools you have seen the enemy use to keep the gospel from spreading, the church from prospering, and Christians from growing?

_____

_____

_____

_____

_____

_____

10. Based on this passage, how should you respond when you sense your plans are being hindered by the enemy? How is Paul's perspective on difficulties helpful to you?

_____

_____

_____

_____

_____

_____

11. Paul expresses his deep desire to visit and comfort the beleaguered Thessalonian believers. Who in your life is embroiled in a great spiritual struggle? How can you help that person?

_____
_____
_____
_____
_____

12. How would you finish this sentence: "My hope, joy, and the crown I will take pride in when Jesus comes is . . ."?

_____
_____
_____
_____
_____

LIFE LESSONS

What happens when we get credible evidence of an impending terrorist attack? Everyone goes on high alert. In every possible way, we ratchet up the level of security. We become wary and vigilant. We take special precautions. We do all these things and more, because the failure to do them could (and likely would) be catastrophic. The same is true in the spiritual realm. We have a despicable, sworn enemy. Satan has declared all-out war on Christ and his church. While the outcome of this cosmic conflict is not in doubt, careless believers can still become casualties of the evil one. Our only hope? To hide ourselves in the God who loves us.

DEVOTION

Lord, make us vigilant today. Remind us that life is war, that we are in the midst of a great cosmic struggle, and that we have an enemy who wants to destroy us. Protect us with your armor and comfort us in our struggles. Arm us today with your wisdom and strength.

JOURNALING

What are some ways to know whether the trials you are facing are coming as a result of Satan's efforts to hinder you to follow God's calling or are just a result of living in a fallen world?

_____

_____

_____

_____

_____

_____

_____

_____

_____

_____

_____

_____

_____

FOR FURTHER READING

To complete the books of 1 and 2 Thessalonians during this twelve-part study, read 1 Thessalonians 2:13–20. For more Bible passages on spiritual warfare, read 2 Corinthians 10:3–5; Ephesians 6:10–19; 1 Timothy 1:18; 6:12; 2 Timothy 2:4; Hebrews 4:12; and 1 Peter 5:8.

ENCOURAGING OTHERS

*Therefore, brothers and sisters, in all our distress
and persecution we were encouraged about you
because of your faith. For now we really live,
since you are standing firm in the Lord.*

2 THESSALONIANS 3:7–8

REFLECTION

Possessions are nice, and abilities are great, but relationships are paramount. After all, could you imagine life without your friends and loved ones? Take a minute to think about the mentors, companions, fellow strugglers, and wise counselors in your life. How have these individuals encouraged you? How have they helped you in your walk with God?

SITUATION

Paul had made every effort to see the believers in Thessalonica, but Satan had blocked his way (see 2 Thessalonians 2:18). So instead, Paul sent his co-worker Timothy to serve in his place and bring back word of their situation. When Timothy made his report, Paul was overjoyed and could only express his thanksgiving for the community. In this next portion of his letter, he encourages the believers to persevere in their faith and stay connected with one another. Paul's words serve as a reminder of how much we also need a strong community of believers around us and what it looks like to lead a life of encouragement.

OBSERVATION

Read 1 Thessalonians 3:1–13 from the New International Version or the New King James Version.

New International Version
[1] So when we could stand it no longer, we thought it best to be left by ourselves in Athens. [2] We sent Timothy, who is our brother and co-worker in God's service in spreading the gospel of Christ, to strengthen and encourage you in your faith, [3] so that no one would be unsettled by these trials. For you know quite well that we are destined for them. [4] In fact, when we were with you, we kept telling you that we would be persecuted. And it turned out that way, as you well know. [5] For this reason, when I could stand it no longer, I sent to find out about your faith. I was afraid that in some way the tempter had tempted you and that our labors might have been in vain.

[6] But Timothy has just now come to us from you and has brought good news about your faith and love. He has told us that you always have pleasant memories of us and that you long to see us, just as we also long to see you. [7] Therefore, brothers and sisters, in all our distress and persecution we were encouraged about you because of your faith. [8] For now we

really live, since you are standing firm in the Lord. [9] How can we thank God enough for you in return for all the joy we have in the presence of our God because of you? [10] Night and day we pray most earnestly that we may see you again and supply what is lacking in your faith.

[11] Now may our God and Father himself and our Lord Jesus clear the way for us to come to you. [12] May the Lord make your love increase and overflow for each other and for everyone else, just as ours does for you. [13] May he strengthen your hearts so that you will be blameless and holy in the presence of our God and Father when our Lord Jesus comes with all his holy ones.

NEW KING JAMES VERSION

[1] Therefore, when we could no longer endure it, we thought it good to be left in Athens alone, [2] and sent Timothy, our brother and minister of God, and our fellow laborer in the gospel of Christ, to establish you and encourage you concerning your faith, [3] that no one should be shaken by these afflictions; for you yourselves know that we are appointed to this. [4] For, in fact, we told you before when we were with you that we would suffer tribulation, just as it happened, and you know. [5] For this reason, when I could no longer endure it, I sent to know your faith, lest by some means the tempter had tempted you, and our labor might be in vain.

[6] But now that Timothy has come to us from you, and brought us good news of your faith and love, and that you always have good remembrance of us, greatly desiring to see us, as we also to see you— [7] therefore, brethren, in all our affliction and distress we were comforted concerning you by your faith. [8] For now we live, if you stand fast in the Lord.

[9] For what thanks can we render to God for you, for all the joy with which we rejoice for your sake before our God, [10] night and day praying exceedingly that we may see your face and perfect what is lacking in your faith?

[11] Now may our God and Father Himself, and our Lord Jesus Christ, direct our way to you. [12] And may the Lord make you increase and abound in love to one another and to all, just as we do to you, [13] so that

He may establish your hearts blameless in holiness before our God and Father at the coming of our Lord Jesus Christ with all His saints.

EXPLORATION

1. Read about Paul's time in Athens in Acts 17:16–34. How does Paul's willingness to be "left by ourselves" (verse 1) and send Timothy back to Thessalonica demonstrate his love for them?

_____

_____

_____

_____

2. For what reason did Paul send his co-worker Timothy back to Thessalonica? Why do you think he chose to send Timothy back at this particular time?

_____

_____

_____

_____

3. Paul notes the believers were destined for trials (see verses 3–4). What does this say about the reality of difficult times in our lives? Why should we not be surprised when they come?

_____

_____

_____

_____

4. What was Paul's great concern when he heard the Thessalonian believers were facing persecution (see verse 5)? What does this say about the way he felt about them?

_____

_____

_____

_____

_____

_____

_____

5. Paul writes, "For now we really live, since you are standing firm in the Lord" (verse 8). Why was it so important to Paul that the Thessalonians were standing firm?

_____

_____

_____

_____

_____

_____

_____

6. Who are the "Pauls and Timothys" in your life—the people who pray for you and exhort you and encourage you? How have they helped you through difficult times?

_____

_____

_____

_____

_____

_____

INSPIRATION

In 1976 tremors devastated the highlands of Guatemala. Thousands of people were killed, and tens of thousands were left homeless. A philanthropist offered to sponsor a relief team from our college. This flyer was posted in our dormitory: "Needed: students willing to use their spring break to build cinder-block homes in Quetzaltenango." I applied, was accepted, and began attending the orientation sessions.

There were twelve of us in all. Mostly ministry students. All of us, it seemed, loved to discuss theology. We were young enough in our faith to believe we knew all the answers. This made for lively discussions. We bantered about a covey of controversies. I can't remember the list. It likely included the usual suspects of charismatic gifts, end times, worship styles, and church strategy. By the time we reached Guatemala, we'd covered the controversies and revealed our true colors. I'd discerned the faithful from the infidels, the healthy from the heretics. I knew who was in and who was out.

But all of that was soon forgotten. The destruction from the earthquake dwarfed our differences. Entire villages had been leveled. Children were wandering through rubble. Long lines of wounded people awaited medical attention. Our opinions seemed suddenly petty. The disaster demanded teamwork. The challenge created a team.

The task turned rivals into partners. I remember one fellow in particular. He and I had distinctly different opinions regarding the styles of worship music. I—the open-minded, relevant thinker—favored contemporary, upbeat music. He—the stodgy, close-minded caveman—preferred hymns and hymnals. Yet when stacking bricks for houses, guess who worked shoulder to shoulder? As we did, we began to sing together. We sang old songs and new, slow and fast. Only later did the irony of it dawn on me. Our common concern gave us a common song.

This was Jesus' plan all along. None of us can do what all of us can do. Remember his commission to the disciples? "You [all of you, collectively] will be my witnesses" (Acts 1:8). Jesus didn't issue individual assignments. He didn't move one by one down the line and knight each individual. . . .

No *I* or *my* or *you*. We are in this together. (From *Outlive Your Life* by Max Lucado.)

REACTION

7. When is a time in your life that a common goal helped you to put aside differences with other believers? Describe the situation.

_____

_____

_____

_____

_____

_____

_____

_____

_____

_____

8. Why do you think God makes it a point that we are to live for him *alongside other believers*?

_____

_____

_____

_____

_____

_____

_____

_____

_____

9. Paul obviously considered Timothy extremely reliable, which is why he sent him to check on the believers in Thessalonica. How does a person develop this quality of dependability?

_____

_____

_____

_____

_____

_____

_____

10. Why is it important to invest your life in other people—not just in projects?

_____

_____

_____

_____

_____

_____

_____

11. When your spiritual leaders reflect on your life, growth, and influence, do you think they rejoice or are discouraged? Why did you answer the way you did?

_____

_____

_____

_____

_____

_____

12. It's been said that everybody needs a spiritual mentor, and everybody needs to mentor someone else. Who fills the roles of the person you mentor and the person who mentors you?

_____

_____

_____

_____

_____

_____

_____

_____

_____

LIFE LESSONS

How easy it is to forget that people are what matter. It's relationships that count. God calls us to a life in community. We are to grow together. We are to serve and minister together. This is the genius of the Christian faith. As we are guided by God's truth, empowered by God's Spirit, and surrounded by God's people, then and only then are we able to finish the race that has been set for us. We need the encouragement of older and wiser saints. We need to be encouraging those new believers that God is calling to himself. We need to be part of a healthy body of believers—committed to doing life together with a band of brothers and sisters.

DEVOTION

Father, Son, and Holy Spirit, keep us from the grave error of thinking that we can lead the Christian life on our own. We need the encouragement of other believers, and they need to be built up by the gifts that you have given to us. May we move closer to others today.

JOURNALING

Who in your world needs some encouragement? Take a few minutes to write out a note of appreciation to that person—and then express those words to him or her this week.

FOR FURTHER READING

To complete the books of 1 and 2 Thessalonians during this twelve-part study, read 1 Thessalonians 3:1–13. For more Bible passages on encouraging others, read Proverbs 10:11; 12:25; 27:17; Romans 12:6–8; Ephesians 4:29; Philippians 2:1; Philemon 1:7; Hebrews 10:23–25; and 1 Peter 4:8–10.

LESSON FIVE

GODLY LIVING

For this is the will of God, your sanctification:
that you should abstain from sexual
immorality. . . . For God did not call
us to uncleanness, but in holiness.
1 THESSALONIANS 4:3,7 NKJV

REFLECTION

The topic of *purity* is one that Christians and church leaders are often reluctant to discuss (except, of course, with teens in a youth group). Yet the apostle Paul never shied away from the subject when he knew his congregations were in danger of falling prey to immorality. What does *purity* mean to you? How have you seen this topic discussed in your church?

_____

_____

_____

_____

_____

_____

_____

_____

_____

_____

_____

_____

_____

_____

_____

_____

SITUATION

Now that Paul has defended his ministry among the Thessalonian believers, he turns to another key purpose of his letter: to urge them to continue living in a manner that is pleasing to the Lord. The believers in Thessalonica, like many other communities Paul had founded, existed in a culture that looked on sexual immortality with indifference or even favor. Paul needed to remind them that they had been *sanctified*—set apart by God—and that the Lord had called them to leave their former ways behind. Furthermore, they were to lead "a quiet life" (1 Thessalonians 4:11) and conduct themselves in a way they won the respect of others.

OBSERVATION

Read 1 Thessalonians 4:1–12 from the New International Version or the New King James Version.

NEW INTERNATIONAL VERSION

[1] As for other matters, brothers and sisters, we instructed you how to live in order to please God, as in fact you are living. Now we ask you and urge you in the Lord Jesus to do this more and more. [2] For you know what instructions we gave you by the authority of the Lord Jesus.

[3] It is God's will that you should be sanctified: that you should avoid sexual immorality; [4] that each of you should learn to control your own body in a way that is holy and honorable, [5] not in passionate lust like the pagans, who do not know God; [6] and that in this matter no one should wrong or take advantage of a brother or sister. The Lord will punish all those who commit such sins, as we told you and warned you before. [7] For God did not call us to be impure, but to live a holy life. [8] Therefore, anyone who rejects this instruction does not reject a human being but God, the very God who gives you his Holy Spirit.

[9] Now about your love for one another we do not need to write to you, for you yourselves have been taught by God to love each other. [10] And in fact, you do love all of God's family throughout Macedonia. Yet we urge you, brothers and sisters, to do so more and more, [11] and to make it your ambition to lead a quiet life: You should mind your own business and

work with your hands, just as we told you,[12] so that your daily life may win the respect of outsiders and so that you will not be dependent on anybody.

New King James Version

[1] Finally then, brethren, we urge and exhort in the Lord Jesus that you should abound more and more, just as you received from us how you ought to walk and to please God; [2] for you know what commandments we gave you through the Lord Jesus.

[3] For this is the will of God, your sanctification: that you should abstain from sexual immorality; [4] that each of you should know how to possess his own vessel in sanctification and honor, [5] not in passion of lust, like the Gentiles who do not know God; [6] that no one should take advantage of and defraud his brother in this matter, because the Lord is the avenger of all such, as we also forewarned you and testified. [7] For God did not call us to uncleanness, but in holiness. [8] Therefore he who rejects this does not reject man, but God, who has also given us His Holy Spirit.

[9] But concerning brotherly love you have no need that I should write to you, for you yourselves are taught by God to love one another; [10] and indeed you do so toward all the brethren who are in all Macedonia. But we urge you, brethren, that you increase more and more; [11] that you also aspire to lead a quiet life, to mind your own business, and to work with your own hands, as we commanded you, [12] that you may walk properly toward those who are outside, and that you may lack nothing.

EXPLORATION

1. Paul states the believers are, in fact, living in a way that pleases the Lord. Given this, why do you think he feels compelled to urge them to do this "more and more" (verse 1)?

_____

_____

_____

_____

2. How would you define the word *sanctification* (see verse 3)?

_____

_____

_____

_____

_____

_____

_____

3. What constitutes *sexual immorality*? Why do you think sexual temptation is so powerful and so problematic for people?

_____

_____

_____

_____

_____

_____

_____

4. What do you think Paul means when he says that anyone he rejects his instruction on personal purity "does not reject a human being but God" (verse 8)?

_____

_____

_____

_____

_____

_____

5. What does Paul say about the way the believers are showing love to one another? Given this, why does he feel compelled to urge them to do this "more and more" (verse 10)?

_____

_____

_____

_____

_____

_____

6. What was Paul advising the believers to do when he said they were to lead "a quiet life" (verse 11)? Why was his purpose in giving this instruction?

_____

_____

_____

_____

_____

_____

_____

INSPIRATION

You're acquainted with house-sitters. You've possibly used one. Not wanting to leave your house vacant, you ask someone to stay in your home until you return. Let me describe two of your nightmares.

The house-sitter redecorates your house. White paint is changed to pink. Berber carpet to shag. An abstract plastic chair sits in the place of your cozy love seat.

His justification? "The house didn't express me accurately. I needed a house that communicated who I am."

Your response? "It's not yours! My residence does not exist to reflect you! I asked you to take care of the house, not take over the house!" Would you want a sitter like this?

You might choose him over nightmare number two. She didn't redecorate; she neglected. Never washed a dish, made a bed, or took out the trash. "My time here was temporary. I knew you wouldn't mind," she explains.

Of course you'd mind! Does she know what this abode cost you?

Both house-sitters made the same mistake. They acted as if the dwelling were theirs. How could they?

Or, better asked, how could we? When it comes to our bodies, the Bible declares that we don't own them. "You are not your own; you were bought at a price. Therefore honor God with your bodies" (1 Corinthians 6:19–20).

Use your body to indulge your passions? To grab attention? To express your opinions? No. Use your body to honor God. "Offer every part of yourself to him as an instrument of righteousness" (Romans 6:13). Your body is God's instrument, intended for his work and for his glory. (From *It's Not About Me* by Max Lucado.)

REACTION

7. How would your thoughts and habits change if you were able to deeply grasp the truth that God owns and lives in *your* body?

_____

_____

_____

_____

_____

_____

_____

_____

8. What does it mean to "offer every part of yourself" to God (Romans 6:13)? How does this extend not only to what you do with your body but also to your thoughts, words, and actions?

_____

_____

_____

_____

9. Paul's principle in this passage in that the Thessalonian believers were doing good—and now should do even better. In what areas do you see your life moving in a positive direction?

_____

_____

_____

_____

10. What warning does Paul give for those who do *not* learn to control their bodies in a way that is holy and honorable?

_____

_____

_____

_____

11. How do you respond to Paul's instruction to lead a quiet and holy life? How do you strive to "mind your own business" in your dealings with others (verse 11)?

_____

_____

_____

_____

12. Why is it important for believers in Christ to live in such a way that wins the respect of even non-believers? How did Paul demonstrate this in his own life?

_____

_____

_____

_____

_____

_____

_____

_____

LIFE LESSONS

Sexual purity is important because sex—like everything else—was created by God and for his glory (see Colossians 1:16). It's crucial to remember that God is *for* sex. He made physical intimacy to be wondrous and pleasurable. He decreed sexual union to be good, when reserved for marriage between a man and woman. He established the sexual act to serve as a physical illustration of the spiritual intimacy and passion creatures can have in knowing their Creator (see Ephesians 5:22–33). Our personal purity is important because any abuse or misuse of this beautiful gift distorts the picture and robs God of the glory that he so richly deserves.

DEVOTION

Father, much like the believers in Paul's day, we live in a sex-saturated and lust-obsessed culture. Grant us today the wisdom to guard our eyes and our hearts. Help us to see sex through your eyes—as beautiful and good—and always strive to honor you with our bodies.

JOURNALING

What are some of the outside influences in your life that project a distorted view of sexuality?

_____

_____

_____

_____

_____

_____

_____

_____

_____

_____

_____

_____

_____

_____

_____

_____

_____

_____

_____

_____

FOR FURTHER READING

To complete the books of 1 and 2 Thessalonians during this twelve-part study, read 1 Thessalonians 4:1–12. For more Bible passages on sexual purity, read Job 31:1; Proverbs 5:20; Matthew 5:28; 1 Corinthians 7:1; Colossians 3:5; Titus 2:5; Hebrews 13:4; and 1 Peter 2:11.

LESSON SIX

THE KING IS COMING!

For the Lord himself will come down from heaven, with a loud command, with the voice of the archangel and with the trumpet call of God, and the dead in Christ will rise first. After that, we who are still alive and are left will be caught up together with them in the clouds.

1 THESSALONIANS 4:16–17

53

REFLECTION

The Second Coming of Christ. The Rapture. Armageddon. Judgment. For centuries, people have been fascinated on the end of the world, and many have even tried to predict when all these events will occur. What are your honest thoughts about this subject? Do you enjoy wondering and studying about the return of Christ? Why or why not?

SITUATION

The return of Christ has been on Paul's mind throughout this letter, as he has urged the believers in Thessalonica to wait for this approaching day and thus escape the "coming wrath" (1 Thessalonians 1:10). Yet Jesus' return was evidently on the believers' minds as well, for part of Timothy's report back to Paul included questions they had about those in the community who had died—and what would happen to them when Jesus made his appearance again into this world. Paul addresses their concerns in this next section of his letter by removing any doubt these believers will somehow "miss out" and not be taken up to heaven along with the living.

OBSERVATION

Read 1 Thessalonians 4:13–5:11 from the New International Version or the New King James Version.

NEW INTERNATIONAL VERSION

4:13 Brothers and sisters, we do not want you to be uninformed about those who sleep in death, so that you do not grieve like the rest of mankind, who have no hope. 14 For we believe that Jesus died and rose again, and so we believe that God will bring with Jesus those who have fallen asleep in him. 15 According to the Lord's word, we tell you that we who are still alive, who are left until the coming of the Lord, will certainly not precede those who have fallen asleep. 16 For the Lord himself will come down from heaven, with a loud command, with the voice of the archangel and with the trumpet call of God, and the dead in Christ will rise first. 17 After that, we who are still alive and are left will be caught up together with them in the clouds to meet the Lord in the air. And so we will be with the Lord forever. 18 Therefore encourage one another with these words.

5:1 Now, brothers and sisters, about times and dates we do not need to write to you, 2 for you know very well that the day of the Lord will come like a thief in the night. ³ While people are saying, "Peace and safety," destruction will come on them suddenly, as labor pains on a pregnant woman, and they will not escape.

⁴ But you, brothers and sisters, are not in darkness so that this day should surprise you like a thief. ⁵ You are all children of the light and children of the day. We do not belong to the night or to the darkness. ⁶ So then, let us not be like others, who are asleep, but let us be awake and sober. ⁷ For those who sleep, sleep at night, and those who get drunk, get drunk at night. ⁸ But since we belong to the day, let us be sober, putting on faith and love as a breastplate, and the hope of salvation as a helmet. ⁹ For God did not appoint us to suffer wrath but to receive salvation through our Lord Jesus Christ. ¹⁰ He died for us so that, whether we are awake or asleep, we may live together with him. ¹¹ Therefore encourage one another and build each other up, just as in fact you are doing.

New King James Version

⁴:¹³ But I do not want you to be ignorant, brethren, concerning those who have fallen asleep, lest you sorrow as others who have no hope. ¹⁴ For if we believe that Jesus died and rose again, even so God will bring with Him those who sleep in Jesus.

¹⁵ For this we say to you by the word of the Lord, that we who are alive and remain until the coming of the Lord will by no means precede those who are asleep. ¹⁶ For the Lord Himself will descend from heaven with a shout, with the voice of an archangel, and with the trumpet of God. And the dead in Christ will rise first. ¹⁷ Then we who are alive and remain shall be caught up together with them in the clouds to meet the Lord in the air. And thus we shall always be with the Lord. ¹⁸ Therefore comfort one another with these words.

⁵:¹ But concerning the times and the seasons, brethren, you have no need that I should write to you. ² For you yourselves know perfectly that the day of the Lord so comes as a thief in the night. ³ For when they say, "Peace and safety!" then sudden destruction comes upon them, as labor pains upon a pregnant woman. And they shall not escape. ⁴ But you,

brethren, are not in darkness, so that this Day should overtake you as a thief. [5] You are all sons of light and sons of the day. We are not of the night nor of darkness. [6] Therefore let us not sleep, as others do, but let us watch and be sober. [7] For those who sleep, sleep at night, and those who get drunk are drunk at night. [8] But let us who are of the day be sober, putting on the breastplate of faith and love, and as a helmet the hope of salvation. [9] For God did not appoint us to wrath, but to obtain salvation through our Lord Jesus Christ, [10] who died for us, that whether we wake or sleep, we should live together with Him.

[11] Therefore comfort each other and edify one another, just as you also are doing.

EXPLORATION

1. In what ways were the believers in Thessalonica evidently "uninformed" about what would happen when Jesus returned to this earth?

_____

_____

_____

_____

_____

_____

2. What does Paul say will happen to those in Christ who have died? What will happen to living Christians when Jesus returns again to this world?

_____

_____

_____

_____

_____

_____

3. Why does Paul state "we believe that Jesus died and rose again" in this discussion (4:14)? What bearing does' Jesus resurrection have on our resurrection (see 1 Corinthians 15:20)?

_____

_____

_____

_____

_____

_____

_____

4. Paul tells the believers about these end-time events so they "do not grieve like the rest of mankind, who have no hope" (4:13). What hope do his words provide for you?

_____

_____

_____

_____

_____

_____

_____

5. What practical difference should the return of Christ make in your life each day?

_____

_____

_____

_____

_____

_____

6. What questions have you had about Jesus' return to this world—when it will occur and how it will happen? What questions do you still have after reading this passage?

_____

_____

_____

_____

_____

_____

INSPIRATION

You are not the only one with questions about death. Listen in on any discussion about the return of Christ, and someone will inquire, "But what about those who have already died? What happens to Christians between their death and Jesus' return?"

Apparently the church in Thessalonica asked such a question. Listen to Paul's words to them: "Brothers and sisters, we do not want you to be uninformed about those who sleep in death, so that you do not grieve like the rest of mankind, who have no hope" (1 Thessalonians 4:13).

The Thessalonian church had buried her share of loved ones. And Paul wants the members who remain to be at peace regarding the ones who have gone ahead. Many of you have buried loved ones as well. And just as God spoke to them, he speaks to you.

If you'll celebrate a marriage anniversary alone this year, he speaks to you.

If your child made it to heaven before making it to kindergarten, he speaks to you.

If you lost a loved one in violence, if you learned more than you want to know about disease, if your dreams were buried as they lowered the casket, God speaks to you.

He speaks to all of us who have stood or will stand in the soft dirt near an open grave. And to us he gives this confident word: "We want you to know what will happen to the believers who have died so you will not grieve like people who have no hope. For since we believe that Jesus died and was raised to life again, we also believe that when Jesus returns, God will bring back with him the believers who have died" (4:13–14 TLB).

God transforms our hopeless grief into hope-filled grief. How? By telling us that we will see our loved ones again. (From *When Christ Comes* by Max Lucado.)

REACTION

7. Who are some of the loved ones you've lost in your lifetime? How do you sense God speaks to all of us who "have stood or will stand in the soft dirt near an open grave"?

_____

_____

_____

_____

_____

_____

8. How do you respond to the idea you do not have to "grieve like people who have no hope" (4:13)? What emotions rise up in you when you read Paul's words in this passage?

_____

_____

_____

_____

_____

_____

9. How do you picture Jesus' return when you read Paul's description in these verses?

_____

_____

_____

_____

_____

_____

10. What do you think Paul means when he says we are "children of the light and of the day; we don't belong to darkness and night" (5:5)?

_____

_____

_____

_____

_____

_____

11. Read Matthew 24:36–41. How does Paul's teaching in this passage agree with Jesus' words? Why do you think God wants you to live in _expectation_ of Jesus' return?

_____

_____

_____

_____

_____

_____

_____

12. How could you use this section of Scripture to help someone who is grieving the death of a loved one? What comfort would this teaching provide?

_____

_____

_____

_____

_____

_____

_____

_____

LIFE LESSONS

Have you ever wondered what that "commanding shout" will be when the Lord returns (see 4:16)? It will be the first audible message most have heard from God. It will be the word that closes one age and opens a new one. It will be the word that puts an end to the sorrows of earth and initiates the joys of heaven for the people of God. Perhaps the King of kings will raise his pierced hand and proclaim, "No more." No more loneliness. No more tears. No more death. No more sadness. No more crying. No more pain. Jesus promised that "the end will come" (Matthew 24:14 NKJV). For those who live for this world, that's bad news. But for those who live for the world to come, it's an encouraging promise.

DEVOTION

Lord Jesus, come quickly! We wait in expectation and long for the day when you will come back again into this world. But whether your return is tomorrow or more than two hundred years from now, let us live in a way that always honors you and points others to you.

JOURNALING

What are some ways you need to change your life to better live in the light, protect yourself with God's armor, and wear the confidence of your salvation (see 1 Thessalonians 5:8)?

FOR FURTHER READING

To complete the books of 1 and 2 Thessalonians during this twelve-part study, read 1 Thessalonians 4:13–5:11. For more Bible passages the return of Christ, read Matthew 24:27–51; 26:64; John 14:1–3; Acts 1:11; Philippians 3:20–21; 1 John 2:28; and Revelation 3:11.

THE CHRISTIAN'S SURVIVAL KIT

Rejoice always, pray without ceasing,
in everything give thanks; for this is the
will of God in Christ Jesus for you.
1 Thessalonians 5:16–18 NKJV

REFLECTION

Pride goes before a fall. A penny saved is a penny earned. Don't do something in the moment you'll regret for a lifetime. We all hear maxims and proverbs like these all the time. What wise sayings or concise bits of advice have had the biggest impact on *your* life? How?

SITUATION

Paul's first letter to the believers in Thessalonica has served to encourage them to persevere in their faith, urge them to continue pursuing a life pleasing to God, and address their fears about what will happen to their loved ones in Christ who have died. Having addressed these concerns, Paul now closes his letter with some basic—but very important—truths the believers need to understand about living as God's people. In particular, Paul reminds them (and us) about what it looks like to live in a Christian community and truly love one another.

OBSERVATION

Read 1 Thessalonians 5:12–28 from the New International
Version or the New King James Version.

NEW INTERNATIONAL VERSION

[12] Now we ask you, brothers and sisters, to acknowledge those who work hard among you, who care for you in the Lord and who admonish you. [13] Hold them in the highest regard in love because of their work. Live in peace with each other. [14] And we urge you, brothers and sisters, warn those who are idle and disruptive, encourage the disheartened, help the weak, be patient with everyone. [15] Make sure that nobody pays back wrong for wrong, but always strive to do what is good for each other and for everyone else.

[16] Rejoice always, [17] pray continually, [18] give thanks in all circumstances; for this is God's will for you in Christ Jesus.

[19] Do not quench the Spirit. [20] Do not treat prophecies with contempt [21] but test them all; hold on to what is good, [22] reject every kind of evil.

[23] May God himself, the God of peace, sanctify you through and through. May your whole spirit, soul and body be kept blameless at the coming of our Lord Jesus Christ. [24] The one who calls you is faithful, and he will do it.

[25] Brothers and sisters, pray for us. [26] Greet all God's people with a holy kiss. [27] I charge you before the Lord to have this letter read to all the brothers and sisters.

[28] The grace of our Lord Jesus Christ be with you.

NEW KING JAMES VERSION

[12] And we urge you, brethren, to recognize those who labor among you, and are over you in the Lord and admonish you, [13] and to esteem them very highly in love for their work's sake. Be at peace among yourselves.

[14] Now we exhort you, brethren, warn those who are unruly, comfort the fainthearted, uphold the weak, be patient with all. [15] See that no one

renders evil for evil to anyone, but always pursue what is good both for yourselves and for all.

¹⁶ Rejoice always, ¹⁷ pray without ceasing, ¹⁸ in everything give thanks; for this is the will of God in Christ Jesus for you.

¹⁹ Do not quench the Spirit. ²⁰ Do not despise prophecies. ²¹ Test all things; hold fast what is good. ²² Abstain from every form of evil.

²³ Now may the God of peace Himself sanctify you completely; and may your whole spirit, soul, and body be preserved blameless at the coming of our Lord Jesus Christ. ²⁴ He who calls you is faithful, who also will do it.

²⁵ Brethren, pray for us.

²⁶ Greet all the brethren with a holy kiss.

²⁷ I charge you by the Lord that this epistle be read to all the holy brethren.

²⁸ The grace of our Lord Jesus Christ be with you. Amen.

EXPLORATION

1. According to Paul, how should Christians view their spiritual leaders and respond to them?

_____

_____

_____

_____

2. Living in peace with other Christians (see verse 13) is a frequent instruction we find in the Bible. What makes this simple command so difficult to live out?

_____

_____

_____

_____

3. What are some ways that even believers can be "idle and disruptive"? How does this correspond to the command to "be patient with everyone" (verse 14)?

_____

_____

_____

_____

4. How is it possible to "rejoice *always*"? What does it mean to "pray *continually*" (verse 16)?

_____

_____

_____

_____

5. What are some ways that you could "quench the Spirit" (verse 19)?

_____

_____

_____

_____

6. Paul has urged his readers to lead sanctified lives. But he now concludes by saying, "May the God of peace Himself sanctify you completely" (verse 23 NKJV). So, how do you become pure—through yourself or through God? How do you resolve this apparent contradiction?

_____

_____

_____

_____

INSPIRATION

When Paul sent Timothy off to spiritual university, he told him to major in the grace of God: "You then, my son, be strong in the grace that is in Christ Jesus" (2 Timothy 2:1). Do the same. Focus on the cross of Christ. Grow fluent in the language of redemption. Linger long at the foot of the cross. Immerse yourself in the curriculum of grace. It's so easy to be distracted. So easy to be ungrateful, to make the mistake of Scott Simpson's caddie.

Scott is a professional golfer who plays often at the Masters Golf Tournament, hosted by the Augusta National Golf Club. Augusta National is to golfers what the Smithsonian is to history buffs: the ultimate experience. The course explodes in beauty. You would think you'd walked into an oil painting. Groomers manicure the course as if she's a wedding-day bride.

In describing the perfection to his caddie, Scott commented, "You won't see a single weed all week." So imagine Scott's surprise when, on Sunday, after five days of walking the course, his caddie pointed to the ground and announced to Scott, "I found one!"

Don't we do the same? We indwell a garden of grace. God's love sprouts around us like lilacs and towers over us like Georgia pines, but we go on weed hunts. How many flowers do we miss in the process?

If you look long enough and hard enough, you'll find something to bellyache about. So quit looking! Lift your eyes off the weeds. Major in the grace of God. And measure the gifts of God. Collect your blessings. Catalog his kindnesses. Assemble your reasons for gratitude and recite them.

"Rejoice always, pray continually, give thanks in all circumstances; for this is God's will for you in Christ Jesus" (1 Thessalonians 5:16–18).

Look at the totality of those terms. *Always be joyful. Pray continually. Give thanks whatever happens.* Learn a lesson from Sidney Connell. When her brand-new bicycle was stolen, she called her dad with the bad news. He expected his daughter to be upset. But Sidney wasn't crying.

She was honored. "Dad," she boasted, "out of all the bikes they could have taken, they took mine."

Gratitude is always an option . . . so major in the grace of God. Measure the gifts of God. Who knows what you might record in your journal?

"Mondays, oh boy—my favorite."

"Tax days, oh boy—my favorite."

"Year-end-review day, oh boy—my favorite."

Impossible, you say? How do you know? How do you know until you give every day a chance? (From *Great Day Every Day* by Max Lucado.)

REACTION

7. How easy or hard is it for you give thanks to God in all situations? In what ways are you more prone to see the "weeds" than the "flowers" in your life?

_____

_____

_____

_____

_____

_____

8. What are some ways you can show greater respect and love to your spiritual leaders—even when you don't always agree with their decisions?

_____

_____

_____

_____

_____

_____

9. On a scale of 1 to 10, with 1 being "hellish" and 10 being "heavenly," how peaceful are your closest relationships right now? What can you do to be more accepting and loving of others?

_____

_____

_____

_____

_____

_____

_____

10. How thankful are you? How can a person develop a more thankful attitude?

_____

_____

_____

_____

_____

_____

_____

11. How does focusing on what Jesus has done for you help you to extend grace to others?

_____

_____

_____

_____

_____

_____

_____

12. Which of these final instructions from Paul is the most pertinent to your life just now? Why?

_____

_____

_____

_____

_____

_____

_____

LIFE LESSONS

Our culture worships at the altars of independence and autonomy. We like to fancy ourselves as "rugged individualists." It would be more accurate to describe us as disconnected and vulnerable. Under the foolish banner of self-sufficiency, millions face life daily without the healthy safeguard of community. The result is loneliness and lives that spin out of control. One of the big lessons of Paul's first letter to the Thessalonians (and the whole Bible, really) is that God made us to be interdependent. We really _do_ need spiritual leaders and fellow strugglers. And others need our encouragement. We were never meant to fly solo. The traveler who ventures out alone has less joy than the one who journeys with some companions. The soldier who fights all by himself is an easy target for the enemy. So . . . where's _your_ community?

DEVOTION

Lord Jesus, thank you for the spiritual leaders you have provided for us and for the brothers and sisters in Christ that you have put into our lives. Help us to grow stronger and deeper and wiser as we participate fully in a healthy community that is devoted to ministry.

JOURNALING

What is a difficult situation you are going through right now that is weighing you down? How can you *choose* to be grateful to God even in this situation and *rejoice always*?

_____

_____

_____

_____

_____

_____

_____

_____

_____

_____

_____

_____

_____

_____

_____

_____

_____

_____

_____

_____

FOR FURTHER READING

To complete the books of 1 and 2 Thessalonians during this twelve-part study, read 1 Thessalonians 5:12–28. For more Bible passages on living a holy life, read Psalm 51:9–10; Isaiah 33:15–16; Romans 12:1–2; 1 Corinthians 6:18; Ephesians 4:17–19; 2 Timothy 2:22; and 1 Peter 1:13–16; 2:9.

LESSON EIGHT

THE UPSIDE
OF TROUBLE

*God is just: He will pay back trouble to
those who trouble you and give relief to
you who are troubled, and to us as well.*

2 THESSALONIANS 1:6–7

REFLECTION

Some people wither and get angry when hard times come, while others seem to get stronger. In the same way, some believers become embittered when they encounter suffering, while others become more like Christ. How can you explain this phenomenon?

_____

_____

_____

_____

_____

_____

_____

_____

_____

_____

_____

_____

_____

_____

_____

_____

_____

_____

SITUATION

After a period of several months, new reports from Thessalonica reached Paul while he and his co-workers were stationed in Corinth. Although conditions in the church remained largely unchanged from the time of Paul's first letter, the believers had more questions for the apostle, which led him to dictate a second letter to the community. Paul opens this letter in much the same way as his first, expressing his thankfulness for the believers and encouraging them to remain faithful to Christ in their times of persecution and suffering.

OBSERVATION

Read 2 Thessalonians 1:1–12 from the New International Version or the New King James Version.

NEW INTERNATIONAL VERSION

1 Paul, Silas and Timothy,

To the church of the Thessalonians in God our Father and the Lord Jesus Christ:

2 Grace and peace to you from God the Father and the Lord Jesus Christ.

3 We ought always to thank God for you, brothers and sisters, and rightly so, because your faith is growing more and more, and the love all of you have for one another is increasing. 4 Therefore, among God's churches we boast about your perseverance and faith in all the persecutions and trials you are enduring.

5 All this is evidence that God's judgment is right, and as a result you will be counted worthy of the kingdom of God, for which you are suffering. 6 God is just: He will pay back trouble to those who trouble you 7 and give relief to you who are troubled, and to us as well. This will happen when the Lord Jesus is revealed from heaven in blazing fire with his powerful angels. 8 He will punish those who do not know God and do not obey the gospel of our Lord Jesus. 9 They will be punished with everlasting destruction and shut out from the presence of the Lord and from the glory of his might 10 on the day he comes to be glorified in his holy people and to be marveled at among all those who have believed. This includes you, because you believed our testimony to you.

¹¹ With this in mind, we constantly pray for you, that our God may make you worthy of his calling, and that by his power he may bring to fruition your every desire for goodness and your every deed prompted by faith. ¹² We pray this so that the name of our Lord Jesus may be glorified in you, and you in him, according to the grace of our God and the Lord Jesus Christ.

New King James Version
¹ Paul, Silvanus, and Timothy,

To the church of the Thessalonians in God our Father and the Lord Jesus Christ:

² Grace to you and peace from God our Father and the Lord Jesus Christ.

³ We are bound to thank God always for you, brethren, as it is fitting, because your faith grows exceedingly, and the love of every one of you all abounds toward each other, ⁴ so that we ourselves boast of you among the churches of God for your patience and faith in all your persecutions and tribulations that you endure, ⁵ which is manifest evidence of the righteous judgment of God, that you may be counted worthy of the kingdom of God, for which you also suffer; ⁶ since it is a righteous thing with God to repay with tribulation those who trouble you, ⁷ and to give you who are troubled rest with us when the Lord Jesus is revealed from heaven with His mighty angels, ⁸ in flaming fire taking vengeance on those who do not know God, and on those who do not obey the gospel of our Lord Jesus Christ. ⁹ These shall be punished with everlasting destruction from the presence of the Lord and from the glory of His power, ¹⁰ when He comes, in that Day, to be glorified in His saints and to be admired among all those who believe, because our testimony among you was believed.

¹¹ Therefore we also pray always for you that our God would count you worthy of this calling, and fulfill all the good pleasure of His goodness and the work of faith with power, ¹² that the name of our Lord Jesus Christ may be glorified in you, and you in Him, according to the grace of our God and the Lord Jesus Christ.

EXPLORATION

1. Paul begins his letter by praising the Thessalonian believers. If your pastor were talking to a fellow minister about you and your church, what specific things would he brag about?

_____

_____

_____

_____

2. What does Paul say about the suffering the believers are facing? What evidence from God does he provide to the church in this passage?

_____

_____

_____

_____

3. Are you shocked when God allows you to go through painful experiences? Why or why not?

_____

_____

_____

_____

4. What is your "theology of suffering"? In other words, how do you reconcile the fact that bad things happen even to those who serve a good and powerful God?

_____

_____

_____

_____

5. Have you ever been persecuted because of your faith? If so, in what ways?

_____

_____

_____

_____

6. Paul tells the believers in Thessalonica that he is constantly praying for them (see verse 11). How would these words—these assurances of prayer—have encouraged you?

_____

_____

_____

_____

INSPIRATION

Since when does the high road lead over a cliff? The answer? Ever since the events of Genesis 3, the chapter that documents the entry of evil into the world. Disaster came in the form of Lucifer, the fallen angel. And as long as Satan "prowls around like a roaring lion" (1 Peter 5:8), he will wreak havoc among God's people.

He will lock preachers, like Paul, in prisons. He will exile pastors, like John, on remote islands. He will afflict the friends of Jesus, like Lazarus, with diseases. But his strategies always backfire. The imprisoned Paul wrote epistles. The banished John saw heaven. The cemetery of Lazarus became a stage upon which Christ performed one of his greatest miracles.

Intended evil becomes ultimate good.

As I reread that promise, it sounds formulaic, catchy, as if destined for a bumper sticker. I don't mean for it to. There is nothing trite about your wheelchair, empty pantry, or aching heart. These are uphill, into-the-wind challenges you are facing. They are not easy.

But neither are they random. God is not *sometimes* sovereign. He is not *occasionally* victorious. He does not occupy the throne one day and vacate it the next. "The Lord shall not turn back until He has executed and accomplished the thoughts and intents of His mind" (Jeremiah 30:24 AMP). This season in which you find yourself may puzzle you, but it does not bewilder God. He can and will use it for his purpose. . . .

Every day God tests us through people, pain, or problems. Stop and consider your circumstances. Can you identify the tests of today? Snarling traffic? Threatening weather? Aching joints?

If you see your troubles as nothing more than isolated hassles and hurts, you'll grow bitter and angry. Yet if you see your troubles as tests used by God for his glory and your maturity, then even the smallest incidents take on significance. (From *You'll Get Through This* by Max Lucado.)

REACTION

7. Why is difficult to view God as *always* sovereign and *always* victorious when negative events come your way? What shift in mindset would be required for you to see your trials this way?

_____

_____

_____

_____

_____

_____

8. How can God possibly be glorified through the suffering of his people? Wouldn't he get more glory out of dramatically rescuing them? Explain.

_____

_____

_____

_____

_____

9. What are some ways that you've sensed God testing you through people, pain, or problems? How have you responded to those events in your life?

_____

_____

_____

_____

_____

10. In what ways have you see prayer make a difference in the lives of those who are suffering?

_____

_____

_____

_____

_____

11. How does the biblical assurance of God's ultimate justice help to make sense of persecution?

_____

_____

_____

_____

_____

12. Should you be concerned if you have never been the recipient of persecution? Why or why not?

_____

_____

_____

_____

_____

_____

_____

LIFE LESSONS

"Everyone who wants to live a godly life in Christ Jesus will be persecuted" (2 Timothy 3:12). Some promise! Not the kind of Bible verse we tend to commit to memory—or to needlepoint and then frame and hang about the living room sofa. And yet, it *is* a divine guarantee. So, what do we do with such a sobering statement? A few suggestions. We can use it to remind ourselves this world is not our home. We can use it to increase our longing for the Lord's return. We can trust that behind such a stark statement stands a God who is always faithful, infinitely powerful, and perfectly good. Whatever we need in times of trial—help, hope, strength—he pledges to supply. His grace is always sufficient. And the next world's rewards to those who persevere through this world's difficulties will far exceed our wildest dreams.

DEVOTION

Father, it is difficult for us to understand suffering, and we are not eager to face persecution. Yet we trust that if and when those times of suffering come into our lives, you are always in control and are always good. All we need in this life we find in you.

JOURNALING

How have you grown in your faith and your relationship with God through struggles and trials?

_____

_____

_____

_____

_____

_____

_____

_____

_____

_____

_____

_____

_____

_____

_____

_____

_____

_____

_____

_____

_____

FOR FURTHER READING

To complete the books of 1 and 2 Thessalonians during this twelve-part study, read 2 Thessalonians 1:1–12. For more Bible passages on suffering, read Matthew 5:11; 10:22,39; Romans 8:17; 2 Corinthians 4:11; Hebrews 11:25; James 5:10; and 1 Peter 2:20; 5:10.

THE GREAT DECEIVER

*Let no one deceive you by any means;
for that Day will not come unless the
falling away comes first, and the man of
sin is revealed, the son of perdition.*

2 THESSALONIANS 2:3 NKJV

REFLECTION

No doubt you've seen that common cartoon character—the somber, bearded man in a white robe, holding a sign that says "Repent! The End Is Near!" Maybe you've even run across such a person in real life. What's your reaction when preachers or Christians start talking about the "end times"? About the devil? About hell?

_____

_____

_____

_____

_____

_____

_____

_____

_____

_____

_____

SITUATION

Paul has opened his second letter to the Thessalonians by expressing his continued thankfulness for them and by reminding them that God will "pay back trouble" to those who have wronged them and "give relief to you who are troubled" (2 Thessalonians 1:6–7). He now addresses a concern that has come to him after hearing the latest report on the community: some of the believers have bought into claims by false teachers that the "day of the Lord" has already arrived. Evidently, a few in the church had even quit their jobs and were waiting for Christ to rescue them from their persecution! Paul addresses this erroneous theological thinking by clarifying what he had taught them and by urging them to live responsibly.

OBSERVATION

Read 2 Thessalonians 2:1–12 from the New International Version or the New King James Version.

NEW INTERNATIONAL VERSION

[1] Concerning the coming of our Lord Jesus Christ and our being gathered to him, we ask you, brothers and sisters, [2] not to become easily unsettled or alarmed by the teaching allegedly from us—whether by a prophecy or by word of mouth or by letter—asserting that the day of the Lord has already come. [3] Don't let anyone deceive you in any way, for that day will not come until the rebellion occurs and the man of lawlessness is revealed, the man doomed to destruction. [4] He will oppose and will exalt himself over everything that is called God or is worshiped, so that he sets himself up in God's temple, proclaiming himself to be God.

[5] Don't you remember that when I was with you I used to tell you these things? [6] And now you know what is holding him back, so that he may be revealed at the proper time. [7] For the secret power of lawlessness is already at work; but the one who now holds it back will continue to do so till he is taken out of the way. [8] And then the lawless one will be revealed, whom the Lord Jesus will overthrow with the breath of his mouth and destroy by the splendor of his coming. [9] The coming of the lawless one will be in accordance with how Satan works. He will use all sorts of displays of power through signs and wonders that serve the lie, [10] and all the ways that wickedness deceives those who are perishing. They perish because they refused to love the truth and so be saved. [11] For this reason God sends them a powerful delusion so that they will believe the lie [12] and so that all will be condemned who have not believed the truth but have delighted in wickedness.

NEW KING JAMES VERSION

[1] Now, brethren, concerning the coming of our Lord Jesus Christ and our gathering together to Him, we ask you, [2] not to be soon shaken in

mind or troubled, either by spirit or by word or by letter, as if from us, as though the day of Christ had come. ³ Let no one deceive you by any means; for that Day will not come unless the falling away comes first, and the man of sin is revealed, the son of perdition, ⁴ who opposes and exalts himself above all that is called God or that is worshiped, so that he sits as God in the temple of God, showing himself that he is God.

⁵ Do you not remember that when I was still with you I told you these things? ⁶ And now you know what is restraining, that he may be revealed in his own time. ⁷ For the mystery of lawlessness is already at work; only He who now restrains will do so until He is taken out of the way. ⁸ And then the lawless one will be revealed, whom the Lord will consume with the breath of His mouth and destroy with the brightness of His coming. ⁹ The coming of the lawless one is according to the working of Satan, with all power, signs, and lying wonders, ¹⁰ and with all unrighteous deception among those who perish, because they did not receive the love of the truth, that they might be saved. ¹¹ And for this reason God will send them strong delusion, that they should believe the lie, ¹² that they all may be condemned who did not believe the truth but had pleasure in unrighteousness.

EXPLORATION

1. What are some of the ways the believers had evidently been deceived concerning the "end times" or the second coming of Christ?

_____

_____

_____

2. What does Paul say has to happen before the arrival of "the day of the Lord" (verses 2–3)?

_____

_____

_____

3. Compare this passage to 1 John 4:2–3 and Revelation 13:1–10. What are the distinguishing characteristics of this "man of lawlessness" who will be revealed (verse 3)?

_____

_____

_____

4. What do these prophecies suggest about the unfolding events of human history?

_____

_____

_____

5. Paul uses words such as *deceive* (verse 3 NKJV), *lying* (verse 9 NKJV), *deception* (verse 10 NKJV), and *delusion* (verse 11) in this passage. What is the message for his readers?

_____

_____

_____

6. Why do you think there is so much confusion, even among Christians, about the "end times"?

_____

_____

_____

INSPIRATION

God has made it clear: the plague of sin will not cross his shores. Infected souls never walk his streets. "Unjust people who don't care about God will not be joining in his kingdom. Those who use and abuse each other, use and abuse sex, use and abuse the earth and everything in it, don't qualify as citizens in God's kingdom" (1 Corinthians 6:9–10 MSG). God refuses to compromise the spiritual purity of heaven.

Herein lies the awful fruit of sin. Lead a godless life, and expect a godless eternity. Spend a life telling God to leave you alone, and he will. He'll grant you an existence "without hope and without God" (Ephesians 2:12). Jesus will "punish those who do not know God and do not obey the gospel of our Lord Jesus. They will be punished with everlasting destruction and shut out from the presence of the Lord and from the glory of his might" (2 Thessalonians 1:8–9).

Christ keeps no secrets about hell. His description purposely chills the soul: A place of darkness (see Matthew 8:12). A fiery furnace (see Matthew 13:42) A place where "the worms . . . do not die, and the fire is not quenched" (Mark 9:48).

Citizens of hell long to die, but cannot. Beg for water, but receive none. They pass into a dawnless night.

So, what can we do? If all have been infected and the world is corrupted, to whom do we turn? Or, to re-ask the great question of Scripture: "What must I do to be saved?" (Acts 16:30). The answer offered then is the answer offered still: "Put your entire trust in the Master Jesus" (Acts 16:31 MSG). (From *Come Thirsty* by Max Lucado.)

REACTION

7. Although the Bible is emphatic that sin is serious, hell is real, and not everyone will be saved, many people still do not believe. Why do you think this is the case?

----

8. The Bible declares a real person called the Antichrist will arise. But even now there is present in the world an "antichrist spirit" (see 1 John 4:3). What are some examples of this spirit?

_____

_____

_____

_____

_____

_____

_____

9. Paul says the "lawless one" will display false miracles, or signs and wonders, that are done through power of the evil one. What is the purpose of these miracles he will perform?

_____

_____

_____

_____

_____

_____

_____

10. Who in your life right now seems especially susceptible to spiritual deception? What can you do to help that person?

_____

_____

_____

_____

_____

_____

11. What are your thoughts as your read this passage from the apostle Paul? Why do you think he went into such detail about the events that would signal the end times?

_____

_____

_____

_____

_____

_____

_____

12. What can and should you do *today* to get ready for the Lord's return?

_____

_____

_____

_____

_____

LIFE LESSONS

At the risk of sounding cheesy, the truth is that history really is His-story. God is in charge of human events. He doesn't wring his hands while wondering what tomorrow holds. He doesn't react to events, scrambling his angels to deal with unexpected emergencies. No. The fact is our Lord has already written the story of the cosmos. "Breaking news" is old hat in heaven. And the ending? That, too, is a settled issue. For us, this means we can relax. We do not have to fret. Our trust (and our souls) are in the good hands of the author, producer, director, and main character of this unfolding drama called real life. And Scripture assures us that by the time of the final curtain, every question will be answered and the plot will be clear to all.

DEVOTION

Father, thank you for the truth that our world is not out of control. You have predetermined how all things will unfold. We praise you for being the Lord of the universe and the King of our hearts.

JOURNALING

Jesus said, "When he, the Spirit of truth, comes, he will guide you into all truth" (John 16:13). How has God's Spirit of truth kept you from falling victim to the lies of the evil one?

FOR FURTHER READING

To complete the books of 1 and 2 Thessalonians during this twelve-part study, read 1 Thessalonians 2:1–12. For more Bible passages on the evil one, read Genesis 3:4–5; Matthew 13:19; John 8:44; 2 Corinthians 4:3–4; Ephesians 6:12; James 4:7; and 1 Peter 5:8–9.

LESSON TEN

STANDING STRONG

So then, brothers and sisters, stand firm and hold fast to the teachings we passed on to you, whether by word of mouth or by letter.
2 Thessalonians 2:15

95

REFLECTION

We all fee a great sense of accomplishment when we persevere and reach a long-term goals. Whether it is operating a profitable business, losing weight, getting into shape, or finally becoming financially healthy, we all like to succeed at what we set out to do. Given this, what do you think causes so many people to *give up* their long-term dreams?

SITUATION

Paul has given the believers in Thessalonica instruction on the "day of the Lord" and how they can know it has not yet occurred. Having addressed this major concern, he now turns the discussion to more practical matters, encouraging the community to hold fast to the teachings he provided when he was with them so they will not be deceived by false teachers. Paul's message to the church and to us is clear: we are to stand firm, resist the temptation to believe what we know is not true, cling stubbornly to the truth, and trust in God's faithfulness.

OBSERVATION

Read 2 Thessalonians 2:13–17 from the New International Version or the New King James Version.

NEW INTERNATIONAL VERSION

[13] But we ought always to thank God for you, brothers and sisters loved by the Lord, because God chose you as firstfruits to be saved through the sanctifying work of the Spirit and through belief in the truth. [14] He called you to this through our gospel, that you might share in the glory of our Lord Jesus Christ.

[15] So then, brothers and sisters, stand firm and hold fast to the teachings we passed on to you, whether by word of mouth or by letter.

[16] May our Lord Jesus Christ himself and God our Father, who loved us and by his grace gave us eternal encouragement and good hope, [17] encourage your hearts and strengthen you in every good deed and word.

NEW KING JAMES VERSION

[13] But we are bound to give thanks to God always for you, brethren beloved by the Lord, because God from the beginning chose you for salvation through sanctification by the Spirit and belief in the truth, [14] to which He called you by our gospel, for the obtaining of the glory of our Lord Jesus Christ. [15] Therefore, brethren, stand fast and hold the traditions which you were taught, whether by word or our epistle.

[16] Now may our Lord Jesus Christ Himself, and our God and Father, who has loved us and given us everlasting consolation and good hope by grace, [17] comfort your hearts and establish you in every good word and work.

EXPLORATION

1. When was the last time you truly sensed that you are loved by the Lord (see verse 13)?

_____

_____

_____

_____

_____

_____

_____

2. Looking back, what are some of the ways God worked in your life to bring you to faith?

_____

_____

_____

_____

_____

_____

_____

3. Paul crams a lot of theology into these few verses. What are some of the reasons he lists as to why Christians can be thankful (see verses 13–14)?

_____

_____

_____

_____

_____

4. What does Paul mean when he instructs the believers to "stand firm" and "hold fast" to the teachings that he passed on to them (verse 15)? What is involved in doing this?

_____

_____

_____

_____

_____

5. What are some ways God encourages and strengthens you?

_____

_____

_____

_____

6. What are some ways you have seen God strengthen you in every good word and deed?

_____

_____

_____

_____

_____

INSPIRATION

Jesus is honest about the life we are called to lead. There is no guarantee that just because we belong to him we will go unscathed. No promise is found in Scripture that says when you follow the king you are exempt from battle. No, often just the opposite is the case.

99

How do we survive the battle? How do we endure the fray? . . . Jesus gives us the assurance of victory: "The one who stands firm to the end will be saved" (Matthew 24:13).

He doesn't say if you succeed you will be saved. Or if you come out on top you will be saved. He says if you endure. An accurate rendering would be, "If you hang in there until the end . . . if you go the distance."

The Brazilians have a great phrase for this. In Portuguese, a person who has the ability to hang in and not give up has *garra*. *Garra* means "claws." What imagery! A person with *garra* has claws which burrow into the side of the cliff and keep him from falling.

So do the saved. They may get close to the edge, they may even stumble and slide. But they will dig their nails into the rock of God and hang on. Jesus gives you this assurance. If you hang on, he'll make sure you get home. . . .

I've been told that during the filming of Ben Hur, Charlton Heston had trouble learning to drive a chariot (who wouldn't?). With much practice he was finally able to control the vehicle, but still had some doubts. He reportedly explained his concerns to the director Cecil B. DeMille by saying, "I think I can drive the chariot, but I'm not sure I can win the race."

DeMille responded, "You just stay in the race and I'll make sure you win." (From *And the Angels Were Silent* by Max Lucado.)

REACTION

7. Jesus said, "The one who stands firm to the end will be saved" (Matthew 24:13). What are some things in believers' lives that make it difficult for them to "stay in the race"?

---

8. Who are some people in your life whom you admire for their ability to persevere? What have you learned from these individuals about endurance?

_____

_____

_____

_____

_____

_____

9. Would you say you are more encouraged or discouraged right now? Why?

_____

_____

_____

_____

_____

_____

10. How would you answer a young Christian who said, "I feel my faith is faltering—what are some practical ways I can continue to believe the teachings of Christ"?

_____

_____

_____

_____

_____

11. Go back through this passage and write down each description you see about God's nature or activity. Spend a moment reflecting on these characteristics. How does this affect you?

_____

_____

_____

_____

_____

12. In what areas of your life do **you** need to stand stronger and persevere more fiercely?

_____

_____

_____

_____

_____

LIFE LESSONS

The most common Greek word translated as _persevere_ in our English Bibles is actually a compound term made up of the Greek verb meaning "to remain" and the prefix "under." In other words, persevering involves "remaining under" a situation. Think of an athlete who bench-presses an enormous weight. It is only under that heavy barbell that he gains muscle and new strength. In the same way, we develop character and faith only when we stay in tough situations. Quitting and running away are the habits of those who never reach their goals or their full potential. Because of Christ, we can do far more than we realize!

DEVOTION

Lord Jesus, forgive our tendency to complain or quit when going gets hard. Teach us to stand strong and persevere. Remind us, as the apostle Paul once prayed, that we "can do all things through Christ" who gives us strength (Philippians 4:13 NKJV).

JOURNALING

How are you living in the reality that you are loved by the Lord? What tasks do you feel he has given you to do? How are you persevering in fulfilling those goals?

FOR FURTHER READING

To complete the books of 1 and 2 Thessalonians during this twelve-part study, read 2 Thessalonians 2:13–17. For more Bible passages on standing firm, read Joshua 23:8; 2 Kings 22:2; Acts 4:19–20; Galatians 5:1; Philippians 1:27; Hebrews 12:1; and Revelation 3:11.

THE IMPORTANCE OF INTERCESSION

Finally, brethren, pray for us, that the word of the Lord may run swiftly and be glorified, just as it is with you.
2 THESSALONIANS 3:1 NKJV

REFLECTION

The statistics on prayer are surprising. An overwhelming majority of people—even irreligious people and even some agnostics—admit to praying at least occasionally. What do you think motivates most of the prayers that people offer to the Lord?

_____

_____

_____

_____

_____

_____

_____

_____

_____

_____

_____

_____

SITUATION

The focus of Paul's second letter has generally been on what scholars call "eschatological" matters—that is, issues concerning Jesus' return, God's judgment on humankind, and the final destination of all true believers in Christ. Paul now concludes his letter with a personal request for them to intercede on his behalf. He has endured much persecution as he has worked to spread the gospel, and he wishes the believers to pray that he will be delivered from those who want to oppose his mission. He also prays the Lord will continue to work in and through them.

OBSERVATION

Read 2 Thessalonians 3:1–5 from the New International Version or the New King James Version.

NEW INTERNATIONAL VERSION

[1] As for other matters, brothers and sisters, pray for us that the message of the Lord may spread rapidly and be honored, just as it was with you. [2] And pray that we may be delivered from wicked and evil people, for not everyone has faith. [3] But the Lord is faithful, and he will strengthen you and protect you from the evil one. [4] We have confidence in the Lord that you are doing and will continue to do the things we command. [5] May the Lord direct your hearts into God's love and Christ's perseverance.

NEW KING JAMES VERSION

[1] Finally, brethren, pray for us, that the word of the Lord may run swiftly and be glorified, just as it is with you, [2] and that we may be delivered from unreasonable and wicked men; for not all have faith.

[3] But the Lord is faithful, who will establish you and guard you from the evil one. [4] And we have confidence in the Lord concerning you, both that you do and will do the things we command you.

[5] Now may the Lord direct your hearts into the love of God and into the patience of Christ.

EXPLORATION

1. What two requests for prayer does Paul make to the Thessalonians in this passage?

_____

_____

_____

_____

2. Why do you think Paul doesn't request more specific prayer for a lessening of his troubles?

_____

_____

_____

_____

_____

3. What percentage of your praying would you say revolves around the spread of the gospel?

_____

_____

_____

_____

4. How consistently do you pray for others? What tends to get in the way of you praying for others on a more regular basis?

_____

_____

_____

_____

5. In this passage, Paul makes several references to the Lord's character. Why is an accurate view of God's nature so essential to having a healthy prayer life?

_____

_____

_____

_____

6. What are your personal prayer habits—the how, what, when, where, and why?

_____

_____

_____

_____

_____

_____

_____

INSPIRATION

The promise of prayer is that *we can change God's mind*. His ultimate will is inflexible, but the implementation of his will is not. He does not change in his character and purpose, but he does alter his strategy because of the appeals of his children. We do not change his intention, but we can influence his actions.

After all, we are ambassadors for Christ (see 2 Corinthians 5:20). Ambassadors represent the king. They speak with the authority of the throne. They carry with them the imprimatur of the one who sent them. If an ambassador sends a request to the king, will the king listen? If you, God's ambassador in this world, come to your King with a request, will he listen? By all means.

You actually have a seat "in the heavenly realms with Christ Jesus" (Ephesians 2:6). You don't have a seat at the Supreme Court or in the House of Representatives. You have one far more strategic; you have a seat in the government of God. Like a congressman you represent a district. You speak on behalf of your family, neighborhood, or softball team. Your sphere of influence is your region. As you grow in faith, your district expands. God burdens you with a concern for orphans, distant lands, or needy people. You respond to these promptings by prayer. *Father . . . they need help. . . .*

Intercessory prayer isn't rocket science. It acknowledges our inability and God's ability. We come with empty hands but high hopes. Why? God "is able to do immeasurably more than all we ask or imagine" (Ephesians 3:20). He will "meet all [our] needs according to the riches of his glory in Christ Jesus" (Philippians 4:19). When God gives, he gives a gift that is "pressed down, shaken together and running over" (Luke 6:38). (From *Before Amen* by Max Lucado.)

REACTION

7. God's will is inflexible, but the implementation of his will is not. How does it impact you to realize you can actually influence God's actions through your prayers?

_____

_____

_____

_____

8. It's been said that God does answer every prayer—with either a *yes*, *no*, or *wait*. How do you typically react when you fail to get a quick *yes* answer from God?

_____

_____

_____

_____

9. Do you think prayer changes your circumstances more or you more? Why?

_____

_____

_____

_____

10. God could have ordered the world in vastly different ways. He certainly doesn't need humans to carry out his will. Why do you think he incorporated this "system" of prayer?

_____

_____

_____

_____

11. What does it mean to be an "ambassador" for Christ? What rights and privileges does that position afford you when it comes to interceding for others?

_____

_____

_____

12. Who are some people whom you could approach about being prayer partners with you?

_____

_____

_____

LIFE LESSONS

A rich prayer life always begins with a right view of God. The person who believes God is uncaring or unfair will never be motivated to seek him. At the same time, the individual who thinks of God as a cosmic genie or celestial Santa Claus will also end up frustrated. But the Christian who sees God as he is—a good, wise, powerful, and always faithful Father—_will_ be eager to pour out his or her heart to God. And here's one more truth: The more deeply we taste his saving and sustaining grace, the more we will pray for others to meet him and experience his life-changing presence and peace.

DEVOTION

Father, thank you for making us ambassadors for Christ and for always hearing our prayers. Today, we ask that you give us a selfless heart for others. Shape us into prayer warriors, always mindful of others, always bringing their needs before your throne.

JOURNALING

Who are three people in your life that are facing struggles and need your intercession? Write out a short prayer for each person in the space below.

_____

_____

_____

_____

_____

_____

_____

_____

_____

_____

_____

_____

_____

_____

FOR FURTHER READING

To complete the books of 1 and 2 Thessalonians during this twelve-part study, read 2 Thessalonians 3:1–5. For more Bible passages on praying for others, read 1 Samuel 7:8; 12:19; 1 Kings 13:6; Romans 15:30; Ephesians 6:19; 1 Timothy 2:1–2; James 5:13–16; and Hebrews 13:18.

LESSON TWELVE

THE VALUE OF WORK

*We worked night and day, laboring and
toiling so that we would not be a burden to
any of you. We did this . . . in order to offer
ourselves as a model for you to imitate.*

2 THESSALONIANS 3:8–9

113

REFLECTION

People in our culture today seem to have a general disdain for work. We see this in the bumper stickers on our cars: "Work fascinates me . . . I can sit and look at it for hours!" "I owe, I owe—it's off to work I go." "Hard work never killed anyone . . . but why take the chance?" Thinking back over your years of employment, what have been your best jobs? Your worst jobs? Why?

_____

_____

_____

_____

_____

_____

_____

_____

_____

_____

_____

_____

_____

SITUATION

As Paul closes his second letter to the believers in Thessalonica, he reiterates they are to avoid any believer who is idle, disruptive, and seeks to turn them from the truth they received when he was with them. He reminds the believers of how he and his coworkers acted when he was in their community and offers their example as a model for the Thessalonians to follow. Instead of being idle "busybodies," they are never to tire of doing what is good and right in God's sight.

OBSERVATION

Read 2 Thessalonians 3:6–18 from the New International Version or the New King James Version.

NEW INTERNATIONAL VERSION

⁶ In the name of the Lord Jesus Christ, we command you, brothers and sisters, to keep away from every believer who is idle and disruptive and does not live according to the teaching you received from us. ⁷ For you yourselves know how you ought to follow our example. We were not idle when we were with you, ⁸ nor did we eat anyone's food without paying for it. On the contrary, we worked night and day, laboring and toiling so that we would not be a burden to any of you. ⁹ We did this, not because we do not have the right to such help, but in order to offer ourselves as a model for you to imitate. ¹⁰ For even when we were with you, we gave you this rule: "The one who is unwilling to work shall not eat."

¹¹ We hear that some among you are idle and disruptive. They are not busy; they are busybodies. ¹² Such people we command and urge in the Lord Jesus Christ to settle down and earn the food they eat. ¹³ And as for you, brothers and sisters, never tire of doing what is good.

¹⁴ Take special note of anyone who does not obey our instruction in this letter. Do not associate with them, in order that they may feel ashamed. ¹⁵ Yet do not regard them as an enemy, but warn them as you would a fellow believer.

¹⁶ Now may the Lord of peace himself give you peace at all times and in every way. The Lord be with all of you.

¹⁷ I, Paul, write this greeting in my own hand, which is the distinguishing mark in all my letters. This is how I write.

¹⁸ The grace of our Lord Jesus Christ be with you all.

NEW KING JAMES VERSION

⁶ But we command you, brethren, in the name of our Lord Jesus Christ, that you withdraw from every brother who walks disorderly and not

according to the tradition which he received from us. ⁷ For you yourselves know how you ought to follow us, for we were not disorderly among you; ⁸ nor did we eat anyone's bread free of charge, but worked with labor and toil night and day, that we might not be a burden to any of you, ⁹ not because we do not have authority, but to make ourselves an example of how you should follow us.

¹⁰ For even when we were with you, we commanded you this: If anyone will not work, neither shall he eat. ¹¹ For we hear that there are some who walk among you in a disorderly manner, not working at all, but are busybodies. ¹² Now those who are such we command and exhort through our Lord Jesus Christ that they work in quietness and eat their own bread.

¹³ But as for you, brethren, do not grow weary in doing good. ¹⁴ And if anyone does not obey our word in this epistle, note that person and do not keep company with him, that he may be ashamed. ¹⁵ Yet do not count him as an enemy, but admonish him as a brother.

¹⁶ Now may the Lord of peace Himself give you peace always in every way. The Lord be with you all.

¹⁷ The salutation of Paul with my own hand, which is a sign in every epistle; so I write.

¹⁸ The grace of our Lord Jesus Christ be with you all. Amen.

EXPLORATION

1. Why do you think Paul commands his readers to "keep away from every believer who is idle and disruptive" (verse 6)? What should be your response to lazy Christians?

---

2. How does Paul describe his own work habits when he was with the believers?

_____

_____

_____

_____

_____

3. Paul actually holds up the way he worked as a model for the believers in Thessalonica to follow. How would your co-workers describe *your* personal work habits?

_____

_____

_____

_____

4. Why does a believer's work ethic matter so much?

_____

_____

_____

_____

5. How do you react to the rule Paul give this congregation: "The one who is unwilling to work shall not eat" (verse 10)? Do you feel it is too strict? Why or why not?

_____

_____

_____

_____

6. Paul provides guidance in this passage on how the believers should confront those who do not obey these words (see verses 14–15). Do you do this? If so, what approach do you take?

_____

_____

_____

_____

_____

_____

INSPIRATION

Many people dread their work. Countless commuters begrudge the 83,000 hours their jobs take from their lives. If you're one of them, what can you do?

Change careers? Perhaps. Find one that better fits your design. But until you change, how do you survive? You still have bills to pay and obligations to meet. The problem might be less the occupation and more the outlook toward. Before you change professions, try this: change your attitude toward your profession.

Jesus' word for frustrated workers can be found in the fifth chapter of Luke's gospel, where we encounter the teacher and the frustrated fisherman. You've likely guessed their names—Jesus and Peter. Random pockets of people populate the Galilean seacoast today. But in the days of Christ, it swarmed, an ant bed of activity. Peter, Andrew, James, and John made their living catching and selling fish. Like other fishermen, they worked the night shift, when cool water brought the game to the surface. And, like other fishermen, they knew the drudgery of a fishless night.

While Jesus preaches, they clean nets. And as the crowd grows, Christ has an idea. "He noticed two boats tied up. The fishermen had just left them and were scrubbing out their nets. He climbed into the boat that was [Peter's] and asked him to put out a little from the shore. Sitting there, using the boat for a pulpit, he taught the crowd" (Luke 5:2–3 MSG).

Jesus claims Peter's boat. He doesn't request the use of it. Christ doesn't fill out an application or ask permission; he simply boards the boat and begins to preach.

He can do that, you know. All boats belong to Christ. Your boat is where you spend your day, make your living, and to a large degree live your life. The taxi you drive, the horse stable you clean, the dental office you manage, the family you feed and transport—this is your boat. Christ shoulder-taps us and reminds:

"You drive my truck."

"You preside in my courtroom." "You work on my job site." "You serve my hospital wing."

To us all, Jesus says, "Your work is my work." (From *Cure for the Common Life* by Max Lucado.)

REACTION

7. How would it change your daily experience if you began seeing your job as a way of serving Christ—as a place to shine for him?

_____

_____

_____

_____

_____

8. Do you think laziness is "contagious"? Why or why not?

_____

_____

_____

_____

9. Arriving late, leaving early, surfing the internet on company time—what are some other common ways Christian workers fail to work in an exemplary fashion?

_____

_____

_____

_____

_____

_____

_____

_____

10. How important is it for parents to teach their children how to work hard and with excellence? Why?

_____

_____

_____

_____

_____

_____

_____

11. What is the right response by a community of faith toward the believer who refuses to support his or her family?

_____

_____

_____

_____

_____

_____

12. What specific changes do you need to make in your work habits?

_____

_____

_____

_____

_____

_____

_____

_____

_____

_____

LIFE LESSONS

Many Christians believe work is evil and part of the divine curse on sin. Not so! God worked in creating the world and called the fruit of his labors *good*. Not only that, but before the fall of humankind, in the perfect environment of Eden, God commissioned Adam to work (see Genesis 2:15). The fact is, when we work with excellence and creativity, we imitate God. As believers, the workplace is one of our primary arenas in which to model the difference Christ makes. Treating co-workers well. Showing respect. Doing what we're told. Meeting deadlines. Going the extra mile. Giving one-hundred percent. Staying focused. Solving problems. Conducting ourselves with integrity. All of these responses provide a great platform for the gospel.

DEVOTION

Father, no matter what we say or claim to believe, if we don't exhibit a changed life in our workplace, our actions only serve as an obstacle to unbelievers. Give us the courage to look closely at our work habits and the grace to bring them in line with your Word.

JOURNALING

What are ten qualities that you think Jesus looks for in a worker?

_____

_____

_____

_____

_____

_____

_____

_____

_____

_____

_____

_____

_____

_____

_____

_____

_____

_____

_____

FOR FURTHER READING

To complete the books of 1 and 2 Thessalonians during this twelve-part study, read 2 Thessalonians 3:6–18. For more Bible passages on being a God-honoring worker, see Genesis 3:19; Proverbs 14:23; 25:13; 27:18; Ecclesiastes 9:10; Ephesians 4:28; Philippians 2:14–15; Colossians 3:23; 1 Timothy 6:1; Titus 2:9; and 1 Peter 2:18.

LEADER'S GUIDE FOR SMALL GROUPS

Thank you for your willingness to lead a group through *Life Lessons from 1 and 2 Thessalonians*. The rewards of being a leader are different from those of participating, and we hope you find your own walk with Jesus deepened by this experience. During the twelve lessons in this study, you will guide your group through selected passages in 1 and 2 Thessalonians and explore the key themes of the letters. There are several elements in this leader's guide that will help you as you structure your study and reflection time, so be sure to follow along and take advantage of each one.

BEFORE YOU BEGIN

Before your first meeting, make sure the group members have their own copy of the *Life Lessons from 1 and 2 Thessalonians* study guide so they can follow along and have their answers written out ahead of time. Alternately, you can hand out the guides at your first meeting and give the group some time to look over the material and ask any preliminary questions. Be sure to send a sheet around the room during that first meeting and have the members write down their name, phone number, and email address so you can keep in touch with them during the week.

There are two ways to structure the duration of the study. You can choose to cover each lesson individually for a total of twelve weeks of discussion, or you can combine two lessons together per week for a total of six weeks of discussion. (Note that if the group members read the selected passages of Scripture for each lesson, they will cover the entire books of 1 and 2 Thessalonians during the study.) The following table illustrates these options:

Twelve-Week Format

Week	Lessons Covered	Reading
1	True Transformation	1 Thessalonians 1:1–10
2	The Question of Motives	1 Thessalonians 2:1–12
3	When Hell Breaks Loose	1 Thessalonians 2:13–20
4	Encouraging Others	1 Thessalonians 3:1–13
5	Godly Living	1 Thessalonians 4:1–12
6	The King Is Coming!	1 Thessalonians 4:13–5:11
7	The Christian's Survival Kit	1 Thessalonians 5:12–28
8	The Upside of Trouble	2 Thessalonians 1:1–12
9	The Great Deceiver	2 Thessalonians 2:1–12
10	Standing Strong	2 Thessalonians 2:13–17
11	The Importance of Intercession	2 Thessalonians 3:1–5
12	The Value of Work	2 Thessalonians 3:6–18

Six-Week Format

Week	Lessons Covered	Reading
1	True Transformation / The Question of Motives	1 Thessalonians 1:1–2:12
2	When Hell Breaks Loose / Encouraging Others	1 Thessalonians 2:13–3:13
3	Godly Living / The King Is Coming!	1 Thessalonians 4:1–5:11
4	The Christian's Survival Kit / The Upside of Trouble	1 Thessalonians 5:12–28; 2 Thessalonians 1:1–12
5	The Great Deceiver / Standing Strong	2 Thessalonians 2:1–17
6	The Importance of Intercession / The Value of Work	2 Thessalonians 3:1–18

Generally, the ideal size you will want for the group is between eight to ten people, which ensures everyone will have enough time to participate in discussions. If you have more people, you might want to break up the main group into smaller subgroups. Encourage those who show up at the first meeting to commit to attending the duration of the study, as this will help the group members get to know each other, create stability for the group, and help you know how to prepare each week.

Each of the lessons begins with a brief reflection that highlights the theme you will be discussing that week. As you begin your group time, have the group members briefly respond to the opening question to get them thinking about the topic at hand. Some people may want to tell a long story in response to one of these questions, but the goal is to keep the answers brief. Ideally, you want everyone in the group to get a chance to answer, so try to keep the responses to just a few minutes. If you have more talkative group members, say up front that everyone needs to limit his or her answer to two minutes.

Give the group members a chance to answer, but tell them to feel free to pass if they wish. With the rest of the study, it's generally not a good idea to have everyone answer every question—a free-flowing discussion is more desirable. But with the opening reflection question, you can go around the circle. Encourage shy people to share, but don't force them.

Before your first meeting, let the group members know how the lessons are broken down. During your group discussion time the members will be drawing on the answers they wrote to the Exploration and Reaction sections, so encourage them to always complete these ahead of time. Also, invite them to bring any questions and insights they uncovered while reading to your next meeting, especially if they had a breakthrough moment or if they didn't understand something they read.

WEEKLY PREPARATION

As the leader, there are a few things you should do to prepare for each meeting:

- *Read through the lesson.* This will help you to become familiar with the content and know how to structure the discussion times.
- *Decide which questions you want to discuss.* Depending on how you structure your group time, you may not be able to cover every question. So select the questions ahead of time that you absolutely want the group to explore.
- *Be familiar with the questions you want to discuss.* When the group meets you'll be watching the clock, so you want to make sure you are familiar with the Bible study questions you have selected. You can then spend time in the passage again when the group meets. In this way, you'll ensure you have the passage more deeply in your mind than your group members.
- *Pray for your group.* Pray for your group members throughout the week and ask God to lead them as they study his Word.
- *Bring extra supplies to your meeting.* The members should bring their own pens for writing notes, but it's a good idea to have extras available for those who forget. You may also want to bring paper and additional Bibles.

Note that in many cases there will not be one "right" answer to the question. Answers will vary, especially when the group members are being asked to share their personal experiences.

STRUCTURING THE DISCUSSION TIME

You will need to determine with your group how long you want to meet each week so you can plan your time accordingly. Generally, most groups like to meet for either sixty minutes or ninety minutes, so you could use one of the following schedules:

Section	60 Minutes	90 Minutes
WELCOME (members arrive and get settled)	5 minutes	10 minutes
REFLECTION (discuss the opening question for the lesson)	10 minutes	15 minutes
DISCUSSION (discuss the Bible study questions in the Exploration and Reaction sections)	35 minutes	50 minutes
PRAYER/CLOSING (pray together as a group and dismiss)	10 minutes	15 minutes

As the group leader, it is up to you to keep track of the time and keep things moving along according to your schedule. You might want to set a timer for each segment so both you and the group members know when your time is up. (Note that there are some good phone apps for timers that play a gentle chime or other pleasant sound instead of a disruptive noise.) Don't feel pressured to cover every question you have selected if the group has a good discussion going. Again, it's not necessary to go around the circle and make everyone share.

Don't be concerned if the group members are silent or slow to share. People are often quiet when they are pulling together their ideas, and this might be a new experience for them. Just ask a question and let it hang in the air until someone shares. You can then say, "Thank you. What about others? What came to you when you reflected on the passage?"

GROUP DYNAMICS

Leading a group through *Life Lessons from 1 and 2 Thessalonians* will prove to be highly rewarding both to you and your group members—but that doesn't mean you will not encounter any challenges along the way! Discussions can get off track. Group members may not be sensitive to the needs and ideas of others. Some might worry they will be expected to talk about matters that make them feel awkward. Others may express comments that result in disagreements. To help ease this strain on you and the group, consider the following ground rules:

- When someone raises a question or comment that is off the main topic, suggest you deal with it another time, or, if you feel led to go in that direction, let the group know you will be spending some time discussing it.
- If someone asks a question you don't know how to answer, admit it and move on. At your discretion, feel free to invite group members to comment on questions that call for personal experience.
- If you find one or two people are dominating the discussion time, direct a few questions to others in the group. Outside the main group time, ask the more dominating members to help you draw out the quieter ones. Work to make them a part of the solution instead of the problem.
- When a disagreement occurs, encourage the group members to process the matter in love. Encourage those on opposite sides to restate what they heard the other side say about the matter, and then invite each side to evaluate if that perception is accurate. Lead the group in examining other Scriptures related to the topic and look for common ground.

When any of these issues arise, encourage your group members to follow the words from the Bible: "Love one another" (John 13:34), "If it is possible, as far as it depends on you, live at peace with everyone" (Romans 12:18), and, "Be quick to listen, slow to speak and slow to become angry" (James 1:19).

Thank you again for taking the time to lead your group. May God reward your efforts and dedication and make your time together in this study fruitful for his kingdom.

ALSO AVAILABLE IN THE LIFE LESSONS SERIES

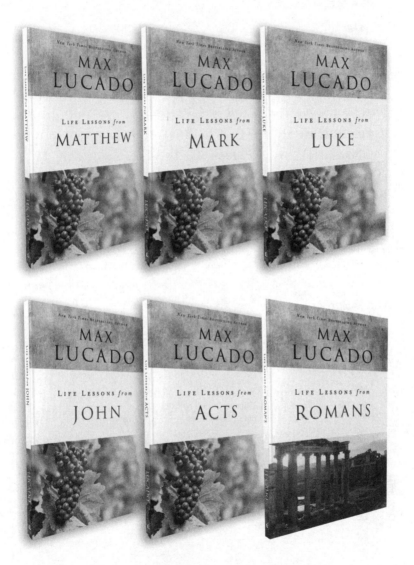

Now available wherever books and ebooks are sold.

Also Available in the Life Lessons Series

Now available wherever books and ebooks are sold.